THE BLACK MAN IN THE LAND OF EQUALITY

THOMAS J. LADENBURG
Lee High School, New Haven

WILLIAM S. McFEELY
Yale University

 HAYDEN BOOK COMPANY, INC., NEW YORK

Acknowledgments:

The authors wish to thank Brett Bissell, Lillian Cohen, Mark Klugheit, Muriel Ladenburg, Ward White, the real John Randolph, and Katherine W. for their generous help in supplying information and ideas used in the writing of this book. The responsibility for its contents is, of course, the writers' alone.

Wherever possible, in the historical sections, eye-witness accounts have been taken from recent reprints available in paperback so that the student can easily pursue the issue further.

Cover Illustrations:

Top — Bettmann Archive, Inc.

Bottom — Susan L. Newman

Preface

No two themes in our country's history stand in sharper contrast than the nation's commitment to equality and the treatment accorded Americans who are black. The dedication to the proposition of equality made in the Declaration of Independence stands challenged by the degradation imposed on black men during their three and a half centuries of life in America. A Swedish scholar, Gunnar Myrdal, observed this contradiction and called attention to it when he titled his study of race relations *An American Dilemma*. His book, published in 1944, was one of the intellectual foundations of the Civil Rights Movement. At this time the nation began confronting the dilemma by reexamining the Negro's place in our society in the light of the historic ideal of equality.

The dilemma remains. There are few domestic issues as compelling to America's citizens as that of race. There is none which is a greater test of the American commitment to democracy. If the test is to be passed it will require a full measure of understanding by all Americans. To achieve this, it makes sense that students — citizens already — face squarely the issue of race in the classroom before encountering it either in the crowded turmoil of the street or the lonely isolation of the voting booth.

The three sections of this book parallel major periods in the history of the Negro in America. Part I examines the myth of the savage African past and goes on to inquire into the institution of slavery. This section raises the question of how his slave past affects the black American's present condition. Part II looks at the Negroes freed in the Civil War. In Reconstruction, the period after the war, equality was not achieved despite promising beginnings. This section raises the question of "how." Is it economic, political, psychological, or legal action which is necessary for an exploited minority people to realize equality in a hostile land? Part III explores the acts of the Civil Rights Movement of our own time and the unrest in the urban ghettoes which remains because those efforts, while bringing us nearer, did not result in equality being reached. The book ends with an examination of two more recent aspects of the ongoing story of the Negro in the land of equality, the drive by black people themselves to achieve Black Power and efforts by the society as a whole to build programs that will compensate for the liabilities imposed on these Americans.

The purpose of this work is to encourage informed judgments by shedding light on controversial issues bearing on race relations. It seeks to replace misconceptions with concepts, to clarify issues by giving illustrative case studies, and to open discussion by presenting problems rather than offering conclusions. The writers — one largely responsible for the historical perspective, the other for the presentation of present-day problems — share a commitment to equality. This has, however, not prevented the presentation of views other than their own, for they wish more to encourage discussion than command agreement. Frank discussion is made possible only by exposure to divergent opinions and truth is seldom served by substituting comfortable myths for unattractive facts. The guiding assumption to this work is that students are perfectly capable of making judgments on controversial issues, that learning increases when conclusions are arrived at rather than imposed, and that the job of the teachers (authors included) is nothing more or less than the encouragement of this inquiry in an atmosphere of mutual respect for free expression.

Table of Contents

PART I

THE NEGRO AS SLAVE

Introduction

Slavery is nasty business. It is also one of the oldest institutions of Western civilization. It existed in Greece and Rome, and if it disappeared in the interior of feudal Europe, it nevertheless flourished in commercial centers on the shores of the continent. Portuguese, Spanish, French, and later Dutch and English commercial fortunes were based largely on the slave trade.

In 1619, a Dutch captain brought into Jamestown, Virginia, the first shipment of "twenty negars" to reach English-speaking America. By the end of the seventeenth century, slaves were an important part of the agricultural labor force in the Carolinas, Virginia, and Maryland. There were also many Negroes in the towns of the middle colonies and, in 1750, Georgia repealed a ban on slavery that had been designed to prevent labor competition with the English debtors who were making a new start in that southern colony. Merchants in Boston and other New England ports grew rich on the slave trade and Southern planters flourished.

The enslavement of Africans in that part of North America which became the United States was, from the start, different from many earlier forms of slavery. The slaves were different from their masters not so much because of their condition of servitude but because they were physically and visibly different. They were black. This was enough to distinguish African slaves from European indentured servants as well. The bonded servants were never bound for life nor were their children born into bondage. Indentured servants were people who were temporarily down-and-out economically; the Africans in America were captive black people whose perpetual slavery ratified their differentness. They were seen as basically unlike and inferior to the white men with whom they were forced to live. In this way, slavery could be justified on the basis of the very inferiorities that were created by black Americans' lack of opportunities for self-development and improvement. Thus Negroes were considered fit for nothing but slavery because they were only allowed to be slaves.

1

In the eighteenth century, some Americans called to conscience by the Quakers and awakened by ideas of the enlightenment began to question the justice of a social order which enslaved other human beings. The ideals of freedom, advanced by the American Revolution, were recognized by some men to be violated by the experiences the Negro slaves were forced to endure. Unluckily, just as this antislavery sentiment was being expounded, politicians who sought to secure the Union, including those who drafted the Constitution, sought to avoid the divisiveness of a national argument over slavery. National programs for gradual emancipation were blocked at a time in which there was widespread antislavery sentiment in the South as well as the North.

A hope that slavery would prove unprofitable and die out proved vain as well. Many crops could be raised effectively with slave labor and the invention of the cotton gin in 1793 firmly entrenched slavery as a Southern institution. By making the mass production of raw cotton possible, this crucial event in the industrial revolution encouraged the textile-manufacture industrialization of England and the mill areas of New England and committed the South to the rule of King Cotton. By 1800, slave-holding in the United States was virtually all in the agricultural South. As the nineteenth century progressed, the new areas of the southwest — Alabama, Mississippi, Louisiana, and Texas — became the sites of huge plantations with thousands of slaves (supplied from the older regions of the east) producing cotton on a large scale.

Whether the slave economy, dependent on staples such as cotton and tobacco, would have continued to prosper forever in the increasingly industrial world of the nineteenth century is still a debated issue. The Virginia legislature came within fifteen votes of providing for the end of slavery in 1831 but, thereafter, the South grew progressively more defensive about the "peculiar institution." Soon Southerners claimed the institution was a positive good and necessary to the continuance of the area's way of life and economic well-being.

By 1860, Americans who wanted to stop the spread of slavery had decided not to wait and see what economics might do. As they correctly observed, the white South was unyielding in its commitment to the preservation of slavery. Nearly 4 million Negroes were subjects of a social system in which they were the chattels (goods, like plows and horses) of another man. Teaching Negroes to read and write was forbidden (a ban which was defied widely — and at great risk). Christianity was used as a means of teaching the slaves obedience and the patience to await rewards in an afterlife. Marriage existed only as permitted by the master. Wives or husbands or children could be sold at any time and sent to any destination or type of work. Many close and friendly observers of the condition of the Negro in America feel that he still labors under social and psychological disabilities acquired under slavery. To learn what life was like under slavery is to gain an understanding of the background of problems faced by black Americans today.

chapter 1

The Negro's African Past

Introduction

The American Negro came to the land of equality in slave ships. He was torn from his native home and packed into boats for shipment to the New World. During a 300-year span, approximately 5 million human beings were transported in chains from Africa to North and South America.

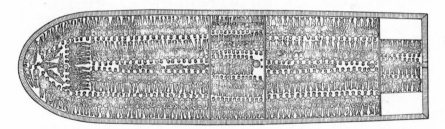

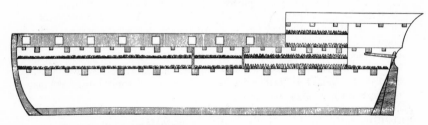

Plan of the slaveship Brookes.

The profits on the slave trade were enormous. An average return was five times the investment, reason enough for the enterprise in the minds of many European and American slave traders, but some justified this traffic in human beings on grounds other than profit. They claimed that blacks benefited by being removed from heathen Africa and brought to Christian America and that life in Africa was so barbaric that even life as a slave in

America was preferable. Though no one today justifies the slave trade, the image of Africa as the land of the bushman, pigmy, or savage lingers on. Indeed, some Americans still consider the American Negro lucky to have escaped his primitive past. This chapter examines the myth of the African past and asks the reader to reevaluate it.

Introducing Oladuah Equiano

Born in Benin, Africa in 1745, Oladuah Equiano was the youngest son of a tribal chief. At age 11, he was captured by Africans, marched hundreds of miles to the coast, and sold to white men. Equiano managed to survive "middle passage," the trip across the Atlantic, and after changing hands several times, became the slave of a British naval officer. But Equiano's experience was somewhat unusual: he was taught to read and write and he was able to earn enough money to purchase his freedom. He set down the story of his life and with the help of English friends found publishers willing to print his account in magazine and book form. His story speaks for the millions of Africans who did not write down their experiences as slaves. Oladuah Equiano's descriptions of his native land stand as testimony to the quality of African life.

Oladuah Equiano's Africa

This kingdom [Benin] is divided into many provinces or districts: in one of the most remote and fertile of which I was born, in the year 1745. . . . The distance of this province from the capital of Benin and the sea coast must be very considerable; for I had never heard of white men or Europeans, nor of the sea; and our subjection to the king of Benin was little more than nominal; for every transaction of the government, as far as my slender observation extended, was conducted by the chiefs or elders of the place. The manners and government of a people who have little commerce with other countries are generally very simple; and the history of what passes in one family or village, may serve as a specimen of the whole nation. My father was one of those elders or chiefs I have spoken of, and was styled Embrenche; a term, as I remember, importing the highest distinction, and signifying in our language a *mark* of grandeur. . . . Those Embrenche, or chief men, decided disputes, and punished crimes; for which purpose they always assembled together. The proceedings were generally short; and in most cases the law of retaliation prevailed. I remember a man was brought before my father, and the other judges, for kidnapping a boy; and, although he was the son of a chief, or senator, he was condemned to make a recompense by a man or woman slave . . .[1]

Economic Life of Oladuah Equiano's Africa

When our women are not employed with the men in tillage, their usual occupation is spinning and weaving cotton, which they afterwards dye, and make into garments. They also manufacture earthen vessels, of which we have many kinds. Among the rest tobacco pipes, made after the same fashion, and used in the same manner, as those in Turkey.

---

[1][Oladuah Equiano], *The Interesting Narrative of the Life of Oladuah Equiano, or Gustavus Vassa, the African,* (Dublin, 1791) pp. 3-5.

Our manner of living is entirely plain; for as yet the natives are un-acquainted with those refinements in cookery which debauch [corrupt] the taste: bullocks, goats, and poultry, supply the greatest part of their food. They constitute likewise the principal wealth of the country, and the chief articles of its commerce. The flesh is usually stewed in a pan. To make it savoury we sometimes use also pepper and other spices; and we have salt made of wood ashes. Our vegetables are mostly plantains, eadas, yams, beans, and Indian corn.

As we live in a country where nature is prodigal of her favors, our wants are few, and easily supplied; of course we have few manufactures. They consist for the most part of calicoes, earthen ware, ornaments, and instru-ments of war and husbandry. But these make no part of our commerce, the principal articles of which, as I have observed, are provisions. In such a state money is of little use; however, we have some small pieces of coin, if I may call them such. They are made something like an anchor; but I do not remember either their value or denomination. We have also markets, at which I have been frequently with my mother. These are sometimes visited by stout mahogany-coloured men from south west of us; we call them *Cye-Eboe,* which term signifies red men living at a distance. They generally bring us firearms, gunpowder, hats, beads, and dried fish. . . . These articles they barter with us for odoriferous [fragrant] woods and earth, and our salt of wood ashes. They always carry slaves through our land; but the strictest account is exacted of their manner of procuring them before they are suffered to pass. . . .

Our land is uncommonly rich and fruitful. . . . Agriculture is our chief employment; and every one, even the children and women, are engaged in it. Thus we are all habituated to labour from our earliest years. Every one contributes something to the common stock; and, as we are unacquainted with idleness we have no beggars. . . .[2]

Customs in Oladuah Equiano's Africa

We are almost a nation of dancers, musicians, and poets. Thus every great event, such as a triumphant return from battle, or other cause of public rejoicing, is celebrated in public dances, which are accompanied with songs and music suited to the occasion. The assembly is separated into four divisions, which dance either apart or in succession, and each with a character peculiar to itself. . . . Each represents some interesting scene of real life, such as a great achievement, domestic employment, a pathetic story, or some rural sport; and as the subject is generally founded on some recent event, it is therefore ever new. This gives our dance a spirit and variety which I have scarcely seen elsewhere. . . .

As our manners are simple, our luxuries are few. The dress of both sexes are nearly the same. It generally consists of a long piece of calico, or muslin, wrapped loosely round the body, somewhat in the form of a high-land plaid. This is usually dyed blue, which is our favourite colour. It is extracted from a berry, and is brighter and richer than I have ever seen in Europe. . . .

The head of a family usually eats alone; his wives and slaves have also their separate tables. Before we taste food, we always wash our hands; indeed our cleanliness on all occasions is extreme; but on this it is an

---

[2]*Ibid.,* pp. 8-9, 12-14.

indispensable ceremony. After washing, libation is made, by pouring out a small portion of the drink on the floor, and tossing a small quantity of the food in a certain place, for the spirits of departed relations, which the natives suppose to preside over their conduct, and guard them from evil. . . .

As to religion, the natives believe that there is one Creator of all things, and that he lives in the sun, and is girded round with a belt, that he may never eat or drink; but according to some, he smokes a pipe, which is our own favourite luxury. They believe he governs events, especially our deaths or captivity; but, as for the doctrine of eternity, I do not remember to have heard of it: some however believe in the transmigration [life in another body] of souls in a certain degree. Those spirits, which are not trans-migrated, such as their dear friends or relations, they believe always attend them, and guard them from the bad spirits of their foes. . . .[8]

Oladuah Equiano in Chains

It was customary in Equiano's village, as in many parts of Africa, for adults to work in the fields and leave the children of the village to play together while one stood guard. If kidnappers happened by, the watchman hopefully would spot them and call for help in time to prevent abduction by other black Africans who were engaged in the business of procuring slaves for sale to the European and American slave ship captains. But it was Equiano's luck to be seized with his sister before either could call for help. The 11-year-old Equiano was bound to fetch a good price.

Though a captive for several months before being delivered to a slave ship, he was completely unprepared for his trip to America:

> The first object which saluted my eyes when I arrived on the coast was the sea, and a slave ship, which was then riding at anchor, and waiting for its cargo. . . . [When I was carried on board] I was immediately handled, and tossed up, to see if I were sound, by some of the crew; and I was now persuaded that I had got into a world of bad spirits, and that they were going to kill me. . . . Indeed, such were the horrors of my views and fears at the moment, that, if ten thousand worlds had been my own, I would have freely parted with them all to have exchanged my condition with that of the meanest slave in my own country. . . . I was soon put down under the decks, and there I received such a salutation in my nostrils as I had never experienced in my life; so that, with the loathsomeness of the stench, and crying together, I became so sick and low that I was not able to eat, nor had I the least desire to taste anything. I now wished for the last friend, Death, to relieve me; but soon to my grief, two of the white men offered me eatables; and, on my refusing to eat, one of them held me fast by the hands, and laid me across, I think, the windlass, and tied my feet, while the other flogged me severely. . . . At last, when the ship we were in had got in all her cargo, they made ready with many fearful noises, and we were all put under deck. . . . The stench of the hold while we were on the coast was so intolerably loathsome, that it was dangerous to remain there for any time. . . . The closeness of the place, and the heat of the climate, added to the number in the ship, which was so crowded that each had scarcely room to turn himself, almost suffocated us. This produced copious perspirations, so that

---

[8]*Ibid.*, pp. 7-9, 18, 20-21.

the air soon became unfit for respiration, from a variety of loathsome smells, and brought on a sickness amongst the slaves, of which many died, thus falling victims to the improvident avarice, as I may call it, of their purchasers. This wretched situation was again aggravated by the galling of the chains, now become insupportable; and the filth of the necessary tubs [privies] into which the children often fell, and were almost suffocated. The shrieks of the women, and the groans of the dying, rendered the whole a scene of horror almost inconceivable. . . .

One day, when we had a smooth sea, and moderate wind, two of my wearied countrymen, who were chained together (I was near them at the time), preferring death to such a life of misery, somehow made through the nettings, and jumped into the sea; immediately another quite dejected fellow also followed their example; and I believe many more would very soon have done the same, if they had not been prevented by the ship's crew, who were instantly alarmed. Those of us that were the most active were in a moment put down under the deck; and there was such a noise and confusion amongst the people of the ship as I never heard before, to stop her, and get the boat out to go after the slaves. However, two of the wretches were drowned, but they got the other, and afterwards flogged him unmercifully, for thus attempting to prefer death to slavery . . .[4]

Oladuah Equiano in the West Indies

The terrible voyage completed, Equiano and the remaining cargo were unloaded in the West Indies and almost immediately placed on the auction block where they were sold to the highest bidder. Equiano noted that these sales separated "relations and friends . . . most of them never to see each other again" and that "it was very moving on this occasion to see and hear their cries at parting." Oladuah Equiano, or Gustavus Vassa, as he was known after he reached Europe, was one of those rare Africans who, brought to America as slaves, were ever to know freedom again. The story of his deliverance from slavery is remarkable but it is the experiences of his less fortunate brothers left behind in America as slaves which we must follow in the next chapter.

QUESTIONS

1. Southerners justified slavery partially on the theory they were rescuing the Negro from barbarism and exposing him to civilization. Evaluate this argument on the basis of what you know of the African past.

2. Negroes today seek to identify with their African heritage. What in fact did Oladuah Equiano have that black men living in the twentieth century may wish to recapture?

---

[4]*Ibid.*, pp. 46-49, 50-53.

SUGGESTED READING

Daniel P. Mannix and Malcolm Cowley's *Black Cargoes, A History of the Atlantic Slave Trade: 1518-1865* (New York, 1962) is a readily available study which draws heavily on contemporary accounts of the operation of the slave trade in Africa. One of the most controversial contributions to the long argument over how much of his cultural heritage survived the slave's middle-passage trip is Melville J. Herskovits' *The Myth of the Negro Past* (Boston, 1941). Herskovits' belief that much was able to survive this ordeal is opposed by Stanley M. Elkins' *Slavery* (New York, 1963), which holds that the trauma of seizure and shipment did basic damage to the Negro's personality.

David Brion Davis's *The Problem of Slavery in Western Culture* (Ithaca, 1966) is a scholarly study of differing Western views of the slave trade, which shaped to both European and American cultural life. Winthrop D. Jordan's *White over Black: American Attitudes Toward the Negro, 1550-1812* is an equally important work which contends that it was the Negro's color and not his condition of servitude which conditioned the prejudice against him.

chapter 2

The Slave As Farm Worker

Introduction

The Southland is a big place, it stretches from Virginia to Texas. In 1850, nearly 9 million people, more than one-third of them Negroes, lived there. The black people, 236,000 of whom were not slaves, worked in a wide range of industries — turpentine and iron were both manufactured with slave labor, for example — and many were house servants or skilled workers in shops in town.

In the remote frontier area, the Negro field hand — perhaps the only one in the county — would work from dawn to dark hoeing the crop with the man who owned him. The long day over, the two men would go back to the farmer's cabin and eat at the same table with the farmer's family. The simple dinner over, the slave would go to his room off the woodshed while his white owner retired to quarters little more luxurious than the Negro's.

The vast majority of slaves, however, were workers on large plantations, supervised by hired overseers rather than by their owners. On these large and often highly organized plantations were raised the great money-crops of the South, most notably cotton.

In 1852, Frederick Law Olmsted, a white Northerner, made an extensive trip through the South reporting for a national audience on what he saw. One native Southerner attested to Olmsted's objectivity, saying: "The general tone of his article is acceptable to unbiased Southerners."[1] Although Olmsted's look at the South was "through a pair of sharp Northern eyes," they were eyes that were wide open. He reported what he saw, not merely what he expected to see. Here is what Olmsted wrote about one visit he made:

> It was a first-rate plantation. On the highest ground stood a large and handsome mansion, but it had not been occupied for several years, and it was more than two years since the overseer had seen the owner. He lived several hundred miles away. . . .

---

[1]Frederick Law Olmsted, *The Slave States,* Harvey Wish, ed. (New York, 1959), p. 12.

The whole plantation, including the swamp land around it, and owned with it, covered several square miles. It was four miles from the settlement to the nearest neighbor's house. There were between thirteen and fourteen hundred acres under cultivation with cotton, corn, and other hoed crops, and two hundred hogs running at large in the swamp. It was the intention that corn and pork enough should be raised to keep the slaves and cattle. . . .[2]

From this description of the plantation, Olmsted moved to a portrait of the slaves and their life.

There were 135 slaves, big and little, of which 67 went to field regularly — equal, the overseer thought, to 60 able-bodied hands. Beside the field hands, there were three mechanics (blacksmith, carpenter, and wheelwright), two seamstresses, one cook, one stable servant, one cattle-tender, one hog-tender, one teamster, one house servant (overseer's cook), and one midwife and nurse. These were all first-class hands; most of them would be worth more, if they were for sale, the overseer said, than the best field hands. There was also a driver of the hoe-gang who did not labor personally, and a foreman of the plow-gang. These two acted as petty officers in the field, and alternately in the quarters.

There was a nursery for sucklings at the quarters, and twenty women at this time who left their work four times each day, for half an hour, to nurse their young ones, and whom the overseer counted as half-hands — that is, expected to do half an ordinary day's work.[3]

Having described the organization of labor on the plantation, Olmsted then discussed the conditions under which the slaves labored, and the hours that were demanded of them. The following description is taken from a dialogue between Olmsted and the overseer of this plantation.

The Plantation Routine

I asked at what time they began working in the morning. "Well," said the overseer, "I do better by my niggers than most. I keep 'em right smart at their work while they do work, but I generally knock 'em off at 8 o'clock in the mornings Saturdays, and give 'em the rest of the day to themselves, and I always gives 'em Sundays, the whole day. Pickin' time, and when the crap's [crop is] bad in grass, I sometimes keep 'em to it till about sunset, Saturdays, but I never work 'em Sundays."

"How early do you start them out in the morning, usually?"

"Well, I don't never start my niggers 'fore daylight 'cept 'tis in pickin' time, then maybe I got 'em out a quarter of an hour before. But I keep 'em right smart to work through the day." He showed an evident pride in the vigilance of his driver, and called my attention to the large areas of ground already hoed over that morning; well hoed, too, as he said.

"At what time do they eat?" I asked. They ate "their snacks" in their cabins, he said, before they came out in the morning (that is before daylight — the sun rising at this time a little before five, and the day dawning, probably, an hour earlier); then at 12 o'clock their dinner was brought to them in a cart — one cart for the plow-gang and one for the hoe-gang. The hoe-gang ate its dinner in the field, and only stopped work long enough to eat it. . . . All worked as late as they could see to work well, and had no more food nor rest until they returned to their cabin. At half past nine o'clock the drivers, each on an alternate night, blew a horn, and at ten visited every cabin to see that its occupants

[2]*Ibid.*, pp. 200-201.
[3]*Ibid.*, p. 201.

were at rest, and not lurking about and spending their strength in fooleries, and
that the fires were safe — a very unusual precaution; the negroes are generally
at liberty after their day's work is done till they are called in the morning.
When washing and patching were done, wood hauled and cut for the fires, corn
ground, etc., I did not learn: probably all chores not of daily necessity, were
reserved for Saturday. Custom varies in this respect. In general, with regard
to fuel for the cabins, the negroes are left to look out for themselves, and they
often have to go to "the swamp" for it, or at least, if it has been hauled, to cut
it to a convenient size, after their day's work is done. The allowance of food
was a peck of corn and four pounds of pork per week, each. When they could
not get "greens" (any vegetables) he generally gave them five pounds of pork.
They had gardens, and raised a good deal for themselves; they also had fowls,
and usually plenty of eggs. He [the overseer] added, "the man who owns this
place does more for his niggers than any other man I know. Every Christmas
he sends me up a thousand or fifteen hundred dollars' [equal to eight or ten
dollars each] worth of molasses and coffee, and tobacco, and calico, and Sunday tricks for 'em. Every family on this plantation gets a barrel of molasses at Christmas." (Not an uncommon practice in Mississippi, though the
quantity is very rarely so generous. It is usually somewhat proportionate to
the value of the last crop sold.)[4]

Olmsted also had the opportunity to observe a black gang at work in the
fields. A black slave gang worked under a black driver, who, in turn,
worked for a white overseer who worked for a white planter; at the same
time, the gang was served by young black girls who acted as "water-toters."
The black drivers often were as fierce as the white overseers; Olmsted
describes one driver who walked among the slaves ". . . with a whip, which
he often cracked at them, sometimes allowing the lash to fall lightly upon
their shoulders. He was constantly urging them also with his voice. All
worked very steadily, and though the presence of a stranger on the
plantation must have been rare, I saw none of them raise or turn their
heads to look at me."[5]

The Cooperative Slave

What was the slave's goal? How much could he determine his role in
the slave society? One way the slave could live was to be what today is
called, derisively, an Uncle Tom. Tom, a fictional character in Harriet
Beecher Stowe's famous novel, *Uncle Tom's Cabin,* was a Negro who won
the respect and love of his white owners for his affectionate and cooperative
attitude toward white men, whose goodwill he sought. The Uncle Tom
of the novel flourished not on a plantation such as the one Olmsted visited,
but rather on a plantation where the master was in residence and took his
fatherly responsibilities seriously.

Even on the plantation Olmsted described, the limited rewards of cooperation were available to the slaves. Beside which, the overseer added, they
were able, if they chose, to buy certain comforts for themselves — tobacco,
for instance — with money earned by Saturday and Sunday work. Some of
them went into the swamps on Sunday and made boards — "puncheons"
made with an ax: "One man sold last year as much as fifty dollars worth."[6]

[4]*Ibid.*, pp. 202-204.
[5]*Ibid.*, p. 202.
[6]*Ibid.*, p. 204.

The Recalcitrant Slave

A second way the slave could cope with his life at long hard work and limited rewards was to work as little as possible. If ability to labor was the only asset the slave had, then to withhold it from the master was to surrender one's self to slavehood less than the cooperative Uncle Tom.

Examples of this are numerous. Olmsted tells of riding out across a plantation one morning with a young man of the planter's family and the overseer. Cutting across an overgrown gully, they came, by chance, on a Negro girl who was hiding in the brush. The overseer accused her of shirking her work in the fields and refused to believe her not very convincing alibis.

> "That won't do;" said he, "get down." The girl knelt on the ground; he got off his horse, and holding the horse with his left hand, struck her [the girl] thirty or forty blows across the shoulders with his tough, flexible, "raw-hide" whip (a terrible instrument for the purpose). . . . At every stroke the girl winced and exclaimed, "Yes, sir!" or "Ah, sir!" or "Please, sir!" not groaning or screaming.

Olmsted then tells how she still refused to give up her story and admit that she was hiding to get away from work, at which the overseer told her to . . .

> ". . . pull up your clothes — lie down." The girl without any hesitation, without a word or look of remonstrance or entreaty, drew closely all her garments under her shoulders, and lay down upon the ground with her face toward the overseer, who continued to flog her with the raw hide, across her naked loins and thighs, with as much strength as before. She now shrunk away from him, not rising, but writhing, groveling, and screaming, "Oh, don't sir! Oh, please stop, master! . . ."
> A young gentleman of fifteen was with us; he had ridden in front, and now, turning on his horse, looked back with an expression only of impatience at the delay.

The overseer, when finished, told Olmsted:

> "She meant to cheat me out of a day's work, and she has done it, too . . . she slipped out of the gang when they were going to work, and she's been dodging about all day. . . ."
> [Olmsted asked] "Was it necessary to punish her so severely?"
> "Oh yes, sir, if I hadn't, she would have done the same thing again to-morrow, and half the people on the plantation would have followed her example. Oh, you've no idea how lazy these niggers are; you Northern people don't know anything about it. They'd never do any work at all if they were not afraid of being whipped."[7]

Escape

A third way for a slave to react to slavery was to escape and become a free man. Some Negroes found their way to freedom on the Underground Railroad, an informally organized network of Northern antislavery white people and free Negroes who passed escaping slaves along to Canada. But it is often forgotten that most slaves who thought of escaping did not live close to the Ohio River or the Mason-Dixon line but instead had hundreds of miles of slave territory to cross if they were to reach free territory. And they

---

[7] *Ibid.*, pp. 275-276.

often had imperfect knowledge of any place other than the plantation on which they very likely had spent their entire lives. "New York they thought lay west of Georgia, and between them and Texas," a Tennessee planter reported.[8] Often, if a slave ran away, it was not to go anywhere in particular, but just because he could no longer tolerate life on his own place.

Olmsted apparently wondered why more slaves did not try to escape. He asked the overseer and received this reply.

> He [the overseer] had no runaways out at this time, but had just sold a bad one to go to Texas. He was whipping this fellow when he turned and tried to stab him — then broke from him and ran away. He had him caught almost immediately by the dogs. After catching him, he kept him in irons until he had a chance to sell him. His niggers did not very often run away, he said, because they were almost sure to be caught. As soon as he saw that one of them was gone he put the dogs on, and if rain had not just fallen, they would soon find him. Sometimes, though, they would outwit the dogs, but if they did they almost always kept in the neighborhood, because they did not like to go where they sometimes could not get back and see their families, and he would soon get wind of where they had been; they would come round to their quarters to see their families and to get food, and as soon as he knew it, he would find their tracks and put the dogs on again. Two months was the longest time any of them ever kept out. They had dogs trained on purpose to run after niggers, and never let out for anything else.[9]

Revolt

A fourth response of the Negroes to slavery — the one most feared by white men all over the South — was a slave revolt. Uprisings did occur, but with great infrequency. In the most famous of these, Nat Turner's Rebellion in 1831, a small band of Virginia Negroes seized guns and killed their masters. The revolt was suppressed and the leaders were killed in reprisal. After this threatening incident, other masters throughout the South kept worried watch and increased their armed patrols at night. There were no further major armed efforts by the Negroes to gain their freedom until the Civil War.

If Olmsted was a Northerner who dealt with slavery in a manner objective enough to render it acceptable to unbiased Southerners, his conclusions should also be of historical import. Having examined slavery in all its varying aspects, Olmsted finally writes:

> It was obvious that all natural incitements to self-advancement had been studiously removed or obstructed, in subordination to the general purpose of making the plantation profitable. The machinery of labor was ungeared during a day and a half of the week, for cleaning and repairs; experience having proved here, as it has in [factories in] Manchester and New York, that operatives do much better work if thus privileged. During this interval, a limited play to individual qualities and impulses was permitted in the culture of such luxuries as potatoes and pumpkins, the repair of garments, and in other sordid recreations involving the least possible intellectual friction.[10]

---

[8]*Ibid.*, p. 211.
[9]*Ibid.*, pp. 201-202.
[10]*Ibid.*, p. 206.

There are many other accounts of life on large plantations in the South, and it is certain that conditions varied greatly. The operation described by Olmsted in such rich detail was undoubtedly a model of efficiency and profitability. Looking at the flourishing plantation that Olmsted has described, what is your impression of the life the Negro slave lived as an agricultural worker?

QUESTIONS

1. Which of the various reactions to the drudgery of the slave's day seem to be the most viable emotional response to slavery?

2. To what extent was punishing the slave girl in the narrative an act of individual cruelty and to what extent was it dictated by the system of slavery?

3. Do working conditions for most Negroes today lend themselves to similar kinds of reactions and responses as the slave's experience elicited?

SUGGESTED READING

Unfortunately, due to the illiteracy of the Negroes involved, there are almost no documents which tell us what we most want to know about slavery — what it was like to be a slave. The most intensive studies of life on the plantations were done by Ulrich B. Phillips, whose racial prejudice should not cause his work to be overlooked. His *American Negro Slavery: A Survey of the Supply, Employment and Control of Negro Labor as Determined by the Plantation Regime* (New York, 1918) is a masterpiece in its genre. The most important recent work on the master-slave relationship is Eugene Genovese's *The Political Economy of Slavery* (New York, 1965).

White Southern diaries and accounts by Northern travelers such as Frederick Law Olmsted's *The Slave States* (New York, 1959) are helpful. Also, Richard Wade's *Slavery in the Cities: the South 1820–1860* (New York, 1964) tells of the slaves who were not living on farms.

chapter 3

The Slave As Family Man

Introduction

As has been noted, many observers contend that the American Negroes' problems in the twentieth century were born in the debilitating environment of slavery in the nineteenth. An eminent sociologist, Daniel P. Moynihan, holds that one of the worst effects of slavery was its legacy of a weak family tradition among black Americans. Marriage was not customarily recognized by American slave holders, as indicated by their common practice of selling fathers away from their wives and children. Mothers, then, were left with the job of directing the family units. Twentieth-century Negro men, unable to obtain jobs as readily as white men or even Negro women, often do not stay with their families and lead them.

According to Moynihan, the dilemma facing disadvantaged Negro families today is that "equality of opportunity almost insures inequality of results."[1] As he sees it,

> At the heart of the deterioration of the fabric of Negro society is the deterioration of the Negro family.
> It is the fundamental source of the weakness of the Negro community at the present time.
> There is probably no single fact of Negro American life so little understood by whites. The Negro situation is commonly perceived by whites in terms of the visible manifestations of discrimination and poverty, in part because Negro protest is directed against such obstacles, and in part, no doubt, because these are the facts which involve the actions and attitudes of the white community as well. It is more difficult, however, for white people to perceive the effect that three centuries of exploitation have had in the fabric of Negro society itself. Here the consequences of the historic injustices done to the Negro Americans are silent and hidden from view. But here is where the true injury has occurred: unless this damage is repaired, all the effort to end discrimination and poverty and injustice will come to little.[2]

---

[1]Office of Policy Planning and Research, United States Department of Labor. *The Negro Family: The Case for National Action* (Washington, 1965), p. 3.
[2]*Ibid.*, p. 5.

Moynihan has a problem explaining how family weakness prior to 1865 can still be limiting the Negroes a hundred years later. (Were there no basic changes in the pattern of family life in the decades after slavery?) Nevertheless, the question this distinguished scholar has raised about the importance of the slaves' family life makes it essential that this aspect of American slavery be examined.

Fanny Kemble

In the 1830's, a glamorous English actress, Fanny Kemble, made a tour of America and took as her prize a rich and lordly South Carolina planter, Pierce Butler. He took her to live on his handsome plantation on the Sea Islands off the Georgia coast. Fanny hated slavery; she told Butler to give it up and, as a family slave reported, "He wouldn't agrees to that, so she goes 'way and she gets a dewoce."[3]

Before she left, she wrote vivid letters about the way the slave families lived. The following is an excerpt from one of them:

These cabins consist of one room, about twelve feet by fifteen, with a couple of closets smaller and closer than the staterooms of a ship, divided off from the main room and each other by rough wooden partitions, in which the inhabitants sleep. They have almost all of them a rude bedstead, with the gray moss of the forests for mattress, and filthy, pestilential-looking blankets, for covering. Two families (sometimes eight and ten in number) reside in one of these huts, which are mere wooden frames pinned, as it were, to the earth by a brick chimney outside, whose enormous aperture within pours down a flood of air, but little counteracted by the miserable spark of fire, which hardly sends an attenuated thread of lingering smoke up its huge throat. A wide ditch runs immediately at the back of these dwellings, which is filled and emptied daily by the tide. Attached to each hovel is a small scrap of ground for a garden, which, however, is for the most part untended and uncultivated. Such of these dwellings as I visited to-day were filthy and wretched in the extreme, and exhibited that most deplorable consequence of ignorance and an abject condition, the inability of the inhabitants to secure and improve even such pitiful comfort as might yet be achieved by them. Instead of the order, neatness, and ingenuity which might convert even these miserable hovels into tolerable residences, there was the careless, reckless, filthy indolence which even the brutes do not exhibit in their lairs and nests, and which seemed incapable of applying to the uses of existence the few miserable means of comfort yet within their reach. Firewood and shavings lay littered about the floors, while the half-naked children were cowering round two or three smouldering cinders. The moss with which the chinks and crannies of their ill-protecting dwellings might have been stuffed was trailing in dirt and dust about the ground, while the backdoor of the huts, opening upon a most unsightly ditch, was left wide open for the fowls and ducks, which they are allowed to raise, to travel in and out, increasing the filth of the cabin, by what they brought and left in every direction. In the midst of the floor, or squatting round the cold hearth, would be four or five little children from four to ten years old, the latter all with babies in their arms, the care of the infants being taken from the mothers (who are driven afield as soon as they recover from child labour), and devolved upon these poor little nurses, as they are called, whose business

---

[3]Willie Lee Rose, *Rehearsal for Reconstruction: The Port Royal Experiment,* (Indianapolis, 1964), p. 112.

it is to watch the infant, and carry it to its mother whenever it may require nourishment. To these hardly human little beings I addressed my remonstrances about the filth, cold, and unnecessary wretchedness of their room, bidding the elder boys and girls kindle up the fire, sweep the floor, and expel the poultry. For a long time my very words seemed unintelligible to them, till, when I began to sweep and make up the fire, etc., they first fell to laughing, and then imitating me.[4]

Of course, it is possible that Fanny Kemble missed the importance that these cabins held for the people who lived in them. Modern-day experiences have taught us something about this in our big cities. Appalled by slum conditions, city planners have leveled many decaying buildings for high-rise replacements. The dreary bug-infested flats have disappeared, but so has the security of life on the block. Too late, it has been discovered that the bad old neighborhood sustains the inhabitant as well as dismaying the observer.

(The Bettmann Archive, Inc.)

It is possible that the slave quarters, dirty and inadequate as they were, served a similar function. The cabin represented relief from the painfully tiring work in the fields. It also was the place where a slave was farthermost from the discipline of the master or overseer. It was in his cabin that he enjoyed whatever family or community life that slavery offered.

---

[4]Frances Anne Kemble, *A Journal & Residence on a Georgian Plantation,* (London, 1863), pp. 32-34.

Slave Marriages

There can be little doubt that human relationships were no less strong because the people that they linked together were slaves. Sometimes marriage rituals were unlike those familiar to us today.

A lifetime after Fanny Kemble described how people lived in the slave huts, old men and women, who had been slaves as children, were interviewed. Here are the recollections, written down in the 1930's, of one man, a former slave, of marriage under slavery:

> Didn't have to ask Marsa or nothin'. Just go to Aunt Sue an' tell her you want to git mated. She tell us to think 'bout it hard fo' two days, cause marrin' was sacred in de eyes of Jesus. After two days Mose an' I went back an' say we done thought 'bout it an' still want to git married. Den she called all de slaves after tasks to pray fo' de union dat God was gonna make. Pray we stay together an' have lots of chillun and none of 'em gets away from de parents. Den she lay a broomstick 'cross de sill of de house we gonna live in an' jine our hands together. Fo' we step over it she ast us once mo' if we was sho' we wanted to git married. 'Course we say yes. Den she say, "In de eyes of Jesus step into Holy land of mat-de-money." When we step 'cross de broomstick, we was married. Was bad luck to tech de broomstick. Fo'ks always stepped high 'cause dey didn't want no spell cast on 'em — Aunt Sue used to say whichever one teched de stick was gonna die fust. . . .

> When you married, you had to jump over a broom three times. Dat was de license. If master seen two slaves together too much he would tell 'em dey was married. Hit didn't make no difference if you wanted to or not; he would put you in de same cabin an' make you live together. . . .

> Marsa used to sometimes pick our wives fo' us. If he didn't have on his place enough women for the men, he would wait on de side of de road till a big wagon loaded with slaves come by. Den Marsa would stop de ole nigger-trader and buy you women. Wasn't no use tryin' to pick one, cause Marsa wasn't gonna pay but so much for her. All he wanted was a young healthy one who looked like she could have children, whether she was purty or ugly as sin. Den he would lead you an' de woman over to one of de cabins and stan' you on de porch. He wouldn't go in. No Sir. He'd stand right dere at de do' an' open de Bible to de first thing he come to an' read somepin real fast out of it. Den he close up de Bible an' finish up wid dis verse:

> > Dat you' wife
> > Dat you' husband
> > I'se you' marsa
> > She you' missus
> > You married.[5]

Mothers and Children

Frequently, family units stayed together for whole lifetimes much as family units did in villages in the North where slavery did not exist. But the possibility always existed that the master, for economic reasons, might break up a family. Here is the way one black woman, a former slave, told about mother-child relationships fostered by the slave system.

> My mother told me that he [the master] owned a woman who was the mother of several children, and when her babies would get about a year or

[5]Milton Meltzer, ed., *In Their Own Words* (New York, 1964), pp. 46-47.

(The Bettmann Archive, Inc.)

two of age he'd sell them, and it would break her heart. She never got to keep them. When her fourth baby was born and was about two months old, she just studied all the time about how she would have to give it up, and one day she said, "I just decided I'm not going to let Old Master sell this baby; he just ain't going to do it." She got up and give it something out of a bottle, and pretty soon it was dead. Of course, didn't nobody tell on her, or he'd of beat her nearly to death.

I heard [a] woman tell how her Mistress said, "Come on, Diana, I want you to go with me down the road a piece." And she went with her, and they got to a place where there was a whole lot of people. They were putting them up on a block and selling them just like cattle. She had a little nursing baby at home and she broke away from her mistress and them and said, "I can't go off and leave my baby." And they had to git some men and throw her down and hold her to keep her from going back to the house. They sold her away from her baby boy. They didn't let her go back to see him again. But she heard from him after he became a young man. Some of her friends that knowed she was sold away from her baby met up with this boy and got to questioning him about his mother. The white folks had told him his mother's name and all. He told them, and they said "Boy, I know your mother. She's down in Newport." And he said, "Gimme her address and I'll write to her and see if I can hear from her." And he wrote. And the white people said they heard such a hollering and shouting going on they said, "What's the matter with Diana?" And they came over to see what was happening. And she said, "I got a letter from my boy that was sold from me when he was a nursing baby." She had me write a letter to him. I did all her writing for her, and he came to see her. I didn't get to see him. I was away when he come. She said she was willing to die that the Lord let her live to see her baby again and take care of him through all these years.[6]

---

[6]B. A. Botkin, ed., *Lay My Burden Down* (Chicago, 1961), pp. 154-155.

In his autobiography, the Negro abolitionist and newspaper editor, Frederick Douglass, relates some of the ambiguities of the slaves' feelings about their relatives.

> . . . My mother was of a darker complexion than either my grandmother or grandfather.
>
> My father was a white man. He was admitted to be such by all I ever heard speak of my parentage. . . . My mother and I were separated when I was but an infant — before I knew her as my mother. It is a common custom in the part of Maryland from which I ran away, to part children from their mothers at a very early age. Frequently, before the child reaches its twelfth month, its mother is taken from it, and hired out on some farm a considerable distance off, and the child is placed under the care of an old woman, too old for field labor. For what this separation is done, I do not know, unless it be to hinder the development of the child's affection toward its mother, and to blunt and destroy the natural affection of the mother for the child. This is the inevitable result.
>
> I never saw my mother, to know her as such, more than four or five times in my life; and each of these times was very short in duration, and at night. She was hired by a Mr. Stewart, who lived about twelve miles from my home. She made her journeys to see me in the night, travelling the whole distance on foot, after the performance of her day's work. She was a field hand, and a whipping is the penalty of not being in the field at sunrise, unless a slave has special permission from his or her master to the contrary — a permission which they seldom get, and one that gives to him that gives it the proud name of being a kind master. I do not recollect of ever seeing my mother by the light of day. She was with me in the night. She would lie down with me, and get me to sleep, but long before I waked she was gone. Very little communication ever took place between us. Death soon ended what little we could have while she lived, and with it her hardships and suffering. She died when I was about seven years old, on one of my master's farms, near Lee's Mill. I was not allowed to be present during her illness, at the death, or burial. She was gone long before I knew any thing about it. Never having enjoyed, to any considerable extent, her soothing presence, her tender and watchful care, I received the tidings of her death with much the same emotion I should have probably felt at the death of a stranger.[7]

Frederick Douglass's recollection of his mother's poignant efforts to remain a mother to him, despite their separation, and his bleak response to her death exposes the great emotional strains endured by black people under slavery. Note that there is no father or husband present to sustain him or his mother. It is this tradition which Moynihan sees as still operating to make life difficult for Negro families in America today.

---

[7]Frederick Douglass, *Narrative of the Life of Frederick Douglass, an American Slave.* (Boston, 1945, New York, 1964), pp. 1-3.

QUESTIONS

1. Could the slave mother be blamed for killing her child or could Frederick Douglass be blamed for not developing stronger family feelings?
2. Given the dependency of the slave — was he in any real way responsible for his attitude toward cleanliness? How could such a cabin be home to its inhabitants?
3. Could the very high illegitimacy and desertion rate among Negroes today be blamed on the family traditions developed under slavery?

SUGGESTED READING

Frederick Douglass's short and brilliant account of his experience as a slave is a most readable and important autobiography of a great American. Published in 1845, it is now available in paperback — Frederick Douglass, *Narrative of the Life of Frederick Douglass, an American Slave* (New York, 1963). Also absorbing reading is B.A. Botkin, ed., *Lay My Burden Down* (Chicago, 1961), a collection of some of the famous interviews with former slaves conducted under the auspices of the Work Progress Administration during the 1930's.

The most important and controversial discussion of the slave legacy of the American Negro family is the "Moynihan Report" prepared by Daniel P. Moynihan and available as *The Negro Family: The Case for National Action* (Washington, 1965).

chapter 4
The Slave Determined To Be Free

Introduction

Born a slave in Maryland in 1817 or 1818, Frederick Douglass escaped from slavery in 1838 and settled in Rochester, New York, where he published the widely read abolitionist newspaper, *Fred Douglass's Paper*. He spoke boldly for abolishing slavery and for equal rights for free Negroes. After the Civil War, he moved to Washington, D.C., and edited the *New Era*. His home on Capitol Hill now houses a collection of African art.

Frederick Douglass.

(The Bettmann Archive, Inc.)

Frederick Douglass was not an ordinary man. Nor was he a typical slave. Certainly, he is one of the few slaves who not only learned to write but did so with great distinction. Hundreds of thousands of field hands found no way to tell us about their lives, but Frederick Douglass did. What follows, in words written soon after his escape, is a portion of his impressions of the "peculiar institution."

Frederick Douglass, Slave

Much of his life, Douglass had lived in relative comfort as a house servant in Baltimore, but when his owner's fortune changed it was necessary to put Douglass to work in the fields. To prepare him for this, he was hired out to Edward Covey, a poor man who rented the farm he operated and made part of his living "breaking" other people's slaves. Covey, "a [Sunday school] class-leader in the Methodist church," took on slaves for a year to break them to the routine of farm work, in return for which his own farm labor was accomplished by the slaves he was training.[1] Here, Frederick Douglass describes Covey's attempt to break him.

I left Master Thomas's house, and went to live with Mr. Covey, on the 1st of January, 1833. I was now, for the first time in my life, a field hand. In my new employment, I found myself even more awkward than a country boy appeared to be in a large city. . . . Mr. Covey sent me, very early in the morning of one of our coldest days in the month of January, to the woods, to get a load of wood. He gave me a team of unbroken oxen. He told me which was the in-hand ox, and which the off-hand one. He then tied the end of a large rope around the horns of the in-hand ox, and gave me the other end of it, and told me, if the oxen started to run, that I must hold on upon the rope. I had never driven oxen before. . . . I had got a very few rods into the woods, when the oxen took fright, and started full tilt, carrying the cart against trees and stumps, in the most frightful manner, I expected every moment that my brains would be dashed out against the trees. After running thus for a considerable distance, they finally upset the cart, dashing it with great force against a tree, and threw themselves into a dense thicket. How I escaped death, I do not know. There I was, entirely alone, in a thick wood, in a place new to me. My cart was upset and shattered, my oxen were entangled among the young trees, and there was none to help me. After a long spell of effort, I succeeded in getting my cart righted, my oxen disentangled, and again yoked to the cart. . . . On my return, I told Mr. Covey what had happened, and how it happened. He ordered me to return to the woods again immediately. I did so, and he followed on after me. Just as I got into the woods, he came up and told me . . . he would teach me how to trifle away my time. . . . He then went to a large gum tree, and with his axe cut three large switches, and, after trimming them up neatly with his pocketknife, he ordered me to take off my clothes. I made him no answer, but stood with my clothes on. He repeated his order. I still made him no answer, nor did I move to strip myself. Upon this he rushed at me with the fierceness of a tiger, tore off my clothes, and lashed me till he had worn out his switches, cutting me so savagely as to leave the marks visible for a long time after. . . .

I lived with Mr. Covey one year. During the first six months, of that year, scarce a week passed without his whipping me. . . . We were worked fully up to the point of endurance. Long before day we were up, our horses fed, and by the first approach of day we were off to the field with our hoes and ploughing teams. Mr. Covey gave us enough to eat, but scarce time to eat it. We

[1]Frederick Douglass, *Narrative of the Life of Frederick Douglass, An American Slave* (New York, 1963), p. 58.

were often less than five minutes taking our meals. We were often in the field from the first approach of day till its last lingering ray had left us; and at saving-fodder time, midnight often caught us in the field binding blades.

"The Snake"

Covey would be out with us. The way he used to stand it, was this. He would spend the most of his afternoon in bed. He would then come out fresh in the evening, ready to urge us on with his words, example, and frequently with the whip. Mr. Covey was one of the few slaveholders who could and did work with his hands. He was a hardworking man. He knew by himself just what a man or a boy could do. There was no deceiving him. His work went on in his absence almost as well as in his presence; and he had the faculty of making us feel that he was ever present with us. This he did by surprising us. He seldom approached the spot where we were at work openly, if he could do it secretly. He always aimed at taking us by surprise. Such was his cunning, that we used to call him, among ourselves, "the snake." . . . His comings were like a thief in the night. He appeared to us as being ever at hand. He was under every tree, behind every stump, in every bush, and at every window on the plantation. . . .

Mr. Covey's *forte* consisted in his power to deceive. . . . He seemed to think himself equal to deceiving the Almighty. He would make a short prayer in the morning, and a long prayer at night; and, strange as it may seem, few men would at times appear more devotional than he. The exercises of his family devotions were always commenced with singing; and, as he was a very poor singer himself, the duty of raising the hymn generally came upon me. He would read his hymn, and nod at me to commence. I would at times do so; at others, I would not. My non-compliance would almost always produce much confusion. To show himself independent of me, he would start and stagger through with his hymn in the most discordant manner. . . .

. . . We were worked in all weathers. It was never too hot or too cold; it could never rain, blow, hail, or snow, too hard for us to work in the field. Work, work, work, was scarcely more the order of the day than of the night. The longest days were too short for him, and shortest nights too long for him. I was somewhat unmanageable when I first went there, but a few months of this discipline tamed me. Mr. Covey succeeded in breaking me. I was broken in body, soul, and spirit. My natural elasticity was crushed, my intellect languished, the disposition to read departed, the cheerful spark that lingered about my eye died; the dark night of slavery closed in upon me; and behold a man transformed into a brute!

"Why Am I a Slave?"

Sunday was my only leisure time. I spent this in a sort of beastlike stupor, between sleep and wake, under some large tree. At times I would rise up, a flash of energetic freedom would dart through my soul, accompanied with a faint beam of hope, that flickered for a moment, and then vanished. I sank down again, mourning over my wretched condition. I was sometimes prompted to take my life, and that of Covey, but was prevented by a combination of hope and fear. . . .

Our house stood within a few rods of the Chesapeake Bay, whose broad bosom was ever white with sails from every quarter of the habitable globe. Those beautiful vessels, robed in purest white, so delightful to the eye of freemen, were to me so many shrouded ghosts, to terrify and torment me with thoughts of my wretched condition. . . . I would pour out my soul's complaint: . . .

"You [ships] are loosed from your moorings, and are free; I am fast in my chains, and am a slave! You move merrily before the gentle gale, and I sadly before the bloody whip. . . . O, why was I born a man, of whom to make a brute! . . . Is there any God? Why am I a slave? I will run away. I will not stand it. Get caught, or get clear, I'll try it. . . . I have only one life to lose. I had as well be killed running as die standing. Only think of it; one hundred miles straight north, and I am free! . . . It cannot be that I shall live and die a slave. I will take to the water. This very bay shall yet bear me into freedom . . . and when I get to the head of the bay, I will turn my canoe adrift, and walk straight through Delaware into Pennsylvania. . . . Let but the first opportunity offer, and, come what will, I am off. Meanwhile, I will try to bear up under the yoke. I am not the only slave in the world. Why should I fret? I can bear as much as any of them. . . . It may be that my misery in slavery will only increase my happiness when I get free. There is a better day coming."

Punishment

. . . On one of the hottest days of the month of August, 1833, Bill Smith, William Hughes, a slave named Eli, and myself, were engaged in fanning wheat. . . . The work was simple, requiring strength rather than intellect; yet, to one entirely unused to such work, it came very hard. About three o'clock of that day, I broke down; my strength failed me; I was seized with a violent aching of the head, attended with extreme dizziness; . . . When I could stand no longer, I fell, and felt as if held down by an immense weight. The fan of course stopped; every one had his own work to do; and no one could do the work of the other, and have his own go on at the same time.

Mr. Covey was at the house. . . . On hearing the fan stop, he . . . came to the spot where we were. . . . I had by this time crawled away under the side of the post and rail-fence by which the yard was enclosed, hoping to find relief by getting out of the sun. [Mr. Covey] gave me a savage kick in the side, and told me to get up. I tried to do so, but fell back in the attempt. . . . While down in this situation, Mr. Covey took up the hickory slat with which Hughes had been striking off the half-bushel measure, and with it gave me a heavy blow upon the head, making a large wound, and the blood ran freely; . . . At this moment I resolved, for the first time, to go to my master, enter a complaint, and ask his protection. In order to do this, I must that afternoon walk seven miles . . . I . . . watched my chance, while Covey was looking in an opposite direction, and started. I succeeded in getting a considerable distance on my way to the woods, when Covey discovered me, and called after me to come back, threatening what he would do if I did not come. I disregarded both his calls and his threats, and made my way to the woods as fast as my feeble state would allow. . . . The blood was yet oozing from the wound on my head. For a time I thought I should bleed to death; and think now that I should have done so, but that the blood so matted my hair as to stop the wound . . . again, and started on my way, through bogs and briers, barefooted and bareheaded, tearing my feet sometimes at nearly every step; and after a journey of about seven miles, occupying some five hours to perform it, I arrived at master's store. . . . He asked me what I wanted. I told him, to let me get a new home; that as sure as I lived with Mr. Covey again, I should live with but to die with him; that Covey would surely kill me; he was in a fair way for it. Master Thomas ridiculed the idea that there was any danger of Mr. Covey's killing me, and said that he knew Mr. Covey; that he was a good man, and that he could not think of taking me from him; that, should he do so, he would lose the whole year's wages; that I belonged to Mr. Covey for one year, and that I must go back to him, come what might; and that I must not trouble him with any more stories, or that he would himself *get hold of me*. After threatening me thus, he gave me a very large dose of salts, telling me that I might remain in St. Michael's that night (it being quite late), but that I must be off back to Mr. Covey's early in the morning. . . . I reached Covey's about nine o'clock;

[in the morning] and just as I was getting over the fence . . . out ran Covey with his cowskin, to give me another whipping. Before he could reach me, I succeeded in getting to the cornfield; and as the corn was very high, it afforded me the means of hiding. He seemed very angry, and searched for me a long time. My behavior was altogether unaccountable. He finally gave up the chase, thinking, I suppose that I must come home for something to eat; he would give himself no further trouble in looking for me. I spent that day mostly in the woods, having the alternative before me, — to go home and be whipped to death, or stay in the woods and be starved to death. That night, I fell in with Sandy Jenkins, a slave with whom I was somewhat acquainted. . . . I found Sandy an old advisor. He told me, with great solemnity, I must go back to Covey; but that before I went, I must go with him into another part of the woods, where there was a certain *root*, which, if I would take some of it with me, carrying it *always on my right side*, would render it impossible for Mr. Covey, or any other white man, to whip me. . . . To please him, I at length took the root, and, according to his direction, carried it upon my right side. This was Sunday morning. I immediately started for home; and upon entering the yard gate, out came Mr. Covey on his way to meeting. He spoke to me very kindly, bade me drive the pigs from a lot near by, and passed on towards the church. . . .

"The Turning Point in My Career"

All went well till Monday morning. On this morning, the virtue of the *root* was fully tested. Long before daylight, I was called to go and rub, curry, and feed, the horses. I obeyed, and was glad to obey. But whilst thus engaged, whilst in the act of throwing down some blades from the loft, Mr. Covey entered the stable with a long rope; and just as I was half out of the loft, he caught hold of my legs, and was about tying me. As soon as I found what he was up to, I gave a sudden spring, and as I did so, he holding to my legs, I was brought sprawling on the stable floor. Mr. Covey seemed now to think he had me, and could do what he pleased; but at this moment — from whence came the spirit I don't know — I resolved to fight; and, suiting my action to the resolution, I seized Covey hard by the throat; and as I did so, I rose. He held on to me, and I to him. My resistance was so entirely unexpected, that Covey seemed taken all aback. . . . He trembled like a leaf. This gave me assurance, and I held him uneasy, causing the blood to run where I touched him with the ends of my fingers. Mr. Covey soon called out to Hughes for help. Hughes came, and, while Covey held me, attempted to tie my right hand. While he was in the act of doing so, I watched my chance, and gave him a heavy kick close under the ribs. This kick fairly sickened Hughes, so that he left me in the hands of Mr. Covey. This kick had the effect of not only weakening Hughes, but Covey also. When he saw Hughes bending over with pain, his courage quailed. He asked me if I meant to persist in my resistance. I told him I did, come what might; that he had used me like a brute for six months, and that I was determined to be used no longer. With that, he strove to drag me to a stick that was lying just out of the stable door. He meant to knock me down. But just as he was leaning over to get the stick, I seized him with both hands by his collar, and brought him by a sudden snatch to the ground. By this time, Bill came. Covey called upon him for assistance. Bill wanted to know what he could do. Covey said, "Take hold of him, take hold of him!" Bill said his master hired him out to work, and not to help to whip me; so he left Covey and myself to fight our own battle out. We were at it for nearly two hours. Covey at length let me go, puffing and blowing at a great rate. . . . The whole six months afterwards, that I spent with Mr. Covey, he never laid the weight of his finger upon me in anger . . . .

This battle with Mr. Covey was the turning point in my career as a slave. It rekindled the few expiring embers of freedom, and revived within me a sense of my own manhood. It recalled the departed self-confidence, and inspired me again with a determination to be free.[2]

Five years later, Douglass escaped from his master.

QUESTIONS

1. Based on the account here, what was the real purpose of sending untrained slaves to a breaker such as Covey?

2. To what do you attribute Douglass's willingness to resist Covey?

3. How, in general terms, can one account for Oladuah Equiano and Frederick Douglass breaking out of slavery while the vast majority of Negroes remained physically and psychologically trapped by the system?

SUGGESTED READING

Frederick Douglass later wrote a full autobiography, but the 1845 account of his life as a slave is the most vivid. Reprinted in paperback (from which the passage in this chapter was taken), it is one of the great stories of our American past: Frederick Douglass, *Narrative of the Life of Frederick Douglass, an American Slave* (New York, 1963). Another exciting story of a slave who escaped and then helped others to find their way to freedom is Dorothy Sterling, *Freedom Train: The Story of Harriet Tubman* (New York, 1954).

---

[2]*Ibid.*, pp. 61-74

chapter 5

Slavery Defended

Introduction

> Nothing is more susceptible to oblivion than an argument, however, ingenious, that has been discredited by events.[1]
>
> Eric L. McKitrick

McKitrick's comment refers in particular to the proslavery arguments made by Southerners in defense of their "peculiar institution." It is McKitrick's belief that the events that took place since emancipation have clearly refuted these arguments. As we have just completed a survey of slavery, we should now be able to examine the white Southern defense of it with a keen, critical eye.

The Argument for Slavery: 1. Negro Inferiority

The defense of slavery took many forms. It typically assumed the Negro to be inferior to his master; the supposed low level of African civilization and the slave's behavior were judged to be unrefutable evidence of this inferiority. The argument failed to consider any African societies higher than those of the cannibals. Africans were regarded as incapable of moral judgments, artistic expression, or refined feelings. Nor did the argument consider that the Negro's behavior may have been determined by his conditioning and his treatment in captivity. Slaves that refused to work for master were considered "lazy." Those too afraid to act manfully were thought "childlike." Those accustomed to master providing the necessities of life were called "improvident." Defenders of slavery were certain these behavior patterns were the results of the natural inferiority of the black man, not the result of his treatment by the white.

The Argument for Slavery: 2. Master and Servant Classes

The defense of slavery took other forms. Southerners like John C. Calhoun held that all societies are divided into master and servant classes,

---

[1]Eric L. McKitrick, *Slavery Defended: The Views of the Old South* (Englewood Cliffs, 1963), p. 1.

and the "inferior" Negro was capable only of being a servant. To prove this division existed in every society, Southerners pointed to the lord and serf of the middle ages, and the factory owner and worker in the North and in other industrialized areas. The relationship between master and slave, the argument ran, was based on this principle of the two-class society. In fact, it was argued, slavery in the South had its counterpart in wage slavery in Northern factories.

This argument did not allow for any classes that were neither workers nor masters. That is, people who owned property as well as worked on it. Nor did it seriously consider the possibility that men born in the lower class should be able to rise to the higher class. The argument condemned man to a station in life determined by the accident of birth, and not by ability or ambition.

The Argument for Slavery: 3. The "Happy" Slave

Since the Negro was considered an inferior human being, and since all societies were felt to divide men into master and slave castes, the slave-holders rationalized that the Negro must be happy in his station as slave — the only position he could fulfill. To further convince themselves of the slave's happiness, Southerners compared his condition to that of other lower-class workers. They discovered that their slaves were much happier than factory workers in either England or America, or than peasants in Ireland or France. In fact, the slave was held to be the happiest working man on the face of the earth. He was happy because his master provided him with all the necessities of life, and he was even happier than his master because he did not have to worry about feeding or sheltering any slaves of his own. This irresponsible and idyllic life of course would not suit the white man, who was capable of thinking and was therefore "fit" for other work, but it pleased the slave, who was not suited for anything else.

The Argument for Slavery: 4. "It's us or them"

The last major defense of slavery to be examined in this chapter rested on a frank appeal to the self-interest of non-slaveholding white Southerners. Many Southerners did not own slaves. They were induced to support slavery by the argument that Negroes and whites could not live as equals under freedom. One race was bound to subjugate the other, and it was far better that the white man should be in the saddle than under it. Though this argument at times relied again on the assumption of Negro inferiority (Negroes were not capable of living under freedom), it occasionally lapsed into the theory that Negroes might overwhelm whites in a struggle for existence. This fear was most intense in areas where black men out-numbered whites, but it was born of more than worry over numerical in-feriority; it suggested a belief in a kind of superiority of the Negroes. The slaves had a submerged but available force of overwhelming physical power. White Southerners who felt this way and claimed that the Negroes would viciously subdue the poor white man, if given a chance at equal opportunity, presented a strange contradiction to their brothers who argued that the docile Negro enjoyed his slave status and would be helpless if freed.

The Development of the Argument for Slavery

Southerners were caught by another strange contradiction in their defense of slavery. During the early days of the Republic the accepted Southern view of slavery held it an unwanted evil forced on the South by alien slave traders. Only the expense of freeing Negroes and the fear of making them equals deterred emancipation. Slavery was viewed as a "necessary evil."

Southerners were frightened by Nat Turner's revolt in 1831 and by the pressure of Northern abolitionists whose efforts might result in black people sharing the South with them without the restraints of slavery. They realized that calling slavery a "necessary evil" was an insufficient defense of the system. They then changed their line of argument, calling their "peculiar institution" a "positive good," a blessing to all mankind, and the only possible way of life consistent with civilized existence. Thomas Jefferson's troubled opposition to slavery was ignored, and Southern leadership of antislavery thought was abandoned. Antislavery literature was banned in the South, abolitionists were equated with Satan, and few Southerners dared attack the institution.

It is understandable that Southerners developed strong defensive arguments to support a system seemingly profitable to the South. After all, white men and not Negroes did the official writing and philosophizing for that section. Because it was in the South's interests to defend slavery, however, does not mean that its arguments were correct, that they squared with the principles of equality on which this nation was founded, or that they developed views of man or society compatible with anything save slavery. For the man who supports slavery or injustice on any grounds manufactures the argument which justifies his own enslavement or the destruction of his own rights.

Governor George McDuffie on Slavery

Governor George McDuffie of South Carolina delivered one of the classic defenses of slavery in a message to his state's legislature in 1835. His message is of particular interest for two reasons. First, it was one of the first public statements of the "positive good" theory of slavery, and, secondly, it contained most of the arguments that were destined to be repeated by Southerners for the next thirty years. Parts of McDuffie's speech are presented below.

Master and Servant Classes

. . . If we look into the elements of which all political communities are composed, it will be found that servitude, in some form, is one of the essential constituents. No community ever has existed without it, and we may confidently assert, none ever will. In the very nature of things there must be classes of persons to discharge all the different offices of society, from the highest to the lowest. Some of those offices are regarded as degrading, though they must and will be performed. Hence the manifold many forms of dependent servitude . . .

The Happy Slave

It is perfectly evident that the destiny of the Negro race is, either the worst possible form of political slavery, or else domestic servitude as it exists in the slaveholding states. The advantage of domestic slavery over the most favorable condition of political slavery, does not admit of a question. It is the obvious interest of the master, not less than his duty, to provide comfortable food and clothing for his slaves; . . . the peasantry and operatives [factory workers] of no country in the world are better provided for, in these respects, than the slaves in our country. In the single empire of Great Britain, the most free and enlightened nation in Europe, there are more wretched paupers and half starving operatives, than there are Negro slaves in the United States. In all respects, the comforts of our slaves are greatly superior to those of the English operatives, or the Irish and continental peasantry;

From . . . excess of labor . . . actual want, and . . . distressing cares, our slaves are entirely exempted. They habitually labor from two to four hours a day less than the operatives in other countries, and it has been truly remarked, by some writer, that a Negro cannot be made to injure himself by excessive labor. It may be safely affirmed that they usually eat as much wholesome and substantial food in one day, as English operatives or Irish peasants eat in two. And as it regards concern for the future, their condition may well be envied, even by their masters. There is not upon the face of the earth, any class of people, high or low, so perfectly free from care and anxiety. They know what their masters will provide for them, under all circumstances, and that in the extremity of old age [last period prior to death] instead of being driven to beggary or to seek public charity in a poor-house, they will be comfortably accommodated and kindly treated among their relatives and associates.

Negro Inferiority

. . . the African Negro is destined by providence to occupy this condition of servile dependence. . . . It is marked on the face, stamped on the skin, and evinced by the intellectual inferiority and natural improvidence of this race. They have all the qualities that fit them for slaves and not one of those that would fit them to be freemen. They are utterly unqualified not only for national freedom, but for self-government of any kind. They are, in all respects, physical, moral, and political, inferior to millions of the human race, who have for consecutive ages dragged out a wretched existence under a grinding political despotism, and who are doomed to this hopeless condition by the very qualities which unfit them for a better. . . .

If the benevolent friends of the black race would compare the condition of that portion of them which we hold in servitude, with that which still remains in Africa, totally unblessed by the lights of civilization or Christianity, and groaning under savage despotism, as utterly destitute of hope as of happiness, they would be able to form some tolerable estimate of what our blacks have lost by slavery in America, and what they have gained by freedom in Africa. Greatly as their condition has been improved by their subjection to an enlighted and Christian people — the only mode under heaven by which it could have been accomplished — they are yet wholly unprepared for anything like a rational system of self-government. . . .

It's "Us or Them"

If emancipated, where would they live and what would be their condition? The idea of their remaining among us is utterly visionary.

Amalgamation [intermarriage] is abhorrent to every sentiment in nature; and if they remain as a separate caste, whether endowed with equal privileges or not, they will become our masters or we must resume the mastery over them. This state of political amalgamation and conflict, which the abolitionists evidently aim to produce, would be the most horrible condition imaginable. . . .[2]

The Slave Response

We have seen the slave system defended by white slave-owners. Yet what of the slave's own view of slavery? It might be interesting to speculate what, for instance, a slave of McDuffie's would have replied to the Governor's arguments. Would he have agreed that he was inferior to his white masters? Would he have accepted their judgment that he was happy in his role as slave?

Unfortunately, we have no such statement by one of McDuffie's slaves, but consider instead the words of Henry Bibb, a black Kentuckian who escaped from slavery. Bibb's master wrote to him in the hope of persuading him to return. He sent his regards, as well, to two other slaves who had escaped. From Michigan, Bibb replied:

Dear Sir:

. . . I am not property now, but am regarded as a man like yourself, and although I live far north, I am enjoying a comfortable living by my own industry.* If you should ever chance to be traveling this way, and will call

Harriet Tubman (extreme left) with ex-slaves she had helped to escape — taken years after the war.   *(The Bettmann Archive, Inc.)*

[2]John A. Scott, ed., *Living Documents in American History* (New York, 1964), pp. 329-32.

*Bibb is here refuting a myth commonly spread among slaves by their masters that if they went North they would surely starve.

on me I will use you better than you did me while you held me as a slave. . . .
As it was the custom of your country to treat your fellow men as you did me
and my little family, I can freely forgive you.

I wish to be remembered in love to my aged mother, and friends. . . .

You wish to be remembered to King and Jack. I am pleased, sir, to inform
you that they are now the owners of better farms than the men who once
owned them.

You may think hard of us for running away from slavery, but as to myself,
I have but one apology to make for it, which is this: I have only to regret that
I did not start at an earlier period. . . . You had it in your power to have kept
me there much longer than you did. I think it is very probable that I should
have been a toiling slave on your property today, if you had treated me
differently.

To be compelled to stand by and see you whip and slash my wife without
mercy, when I could offer her no protection, not even by offering myself to
suffer the lash in her place, was more than I felt it to be the duty of a slave
husband to endure. . . . This kind of treatment was what drove me from
home and family, to seek a better home for them.[3]

To Henry Bibb then, as certainly to Nat Turner, Frederick Douglass, and
others before them, slavery was neither a necessary evil nor a positive good.

QUESTIONS

1. In what ways did slaves seem inferior to most Southerners? Based on
the material covered in this unit, could you explain why?
2. Why did the "happy slave" and the "master and servant class" arguments
depend on the assumption of Negro inferiority? Evaluate these arguments.
3. Approximately 80 per cent of all Southerners did not own slaves and yet
most Southerners were vehement in their defense of slavery. Which of
the proslave arguments do you think appealed most to them? Why?

SUGGESTED READING

The best way to sample the rhetoric of the proslavery cause is to obtain
the paperback, Eric L. McKitrick, ed., *Slavery Defended: The Views of
the Old South* (Englewood Cliffs, 1963). The classic document of the genre
is George Fitzhugh, *Cannibals All!* (Richmond, 1857).

One of the most interesting attacks on slavery was written by a Southerner
no fonder of the Negro than Fitzhugh. Hinton R. Helper's *The Impending
Crisis of the South: And How to Meet it* (New York, 1857) holds that
Negro slavery impeded the advance of independent white farmers. Much
more sophisticated than often thought — and certainly kinder in its view
of the Negro — is Harriet Beecher Stowe's *Uncle Tom's Cabin* published
in 1852 and now available in many paperback editions.

---

[3]Herbert Aptheker, ed., *A Documentary History of the Negro People in the
United States* (New York, 1962), pp. 237-238.

PART II.
THE NEGRO AS FREEDMAN

Introduction

The Civil War was the way Americans ended slavery in their society. The war began as a fight to save the Union. When the forcible return of the seceded South proved more difficult than expected, President Lincoln signed the Emancipation Proclamation to assist the military effort. The executive order was designed to demoralize the Confederacy, to appease antislavery elements in England, and to encourage the enlistment of Negro troops. The last of these objectives is the one which can be demonstrated to have been the most successful. Two hundred thousand Negro soldiers fought in the Union Army during the war.

If Lincoln's first concern was always the salvation of the Union, there were some Americans who did not think the Union worth saving if slavery were not ended. Abolitionists had exerted great pressure on the President to turn the war into a crusade against slavery. They succeeded on January 1, 1863, when the Emancipation Proclamation went into effect. Unfortunately, not all of these abolitionists cared as much about the Negroes who were slaves as they did about purging a white nation of the sin of black slavery. But those who did, along with other thoughtful Americans, began to consider how countless free Negroes who had known how to live only under the discipline of slavery would fare in an America in which slavery did not exist.

Once they were no longer slaves, would the Negroes, like all other men, be considered to have been "created equal" as Thomas Jefferson had said they were? That phrase, written into the Declaration of Independence by the Virginia slaveowner, has troubled Americans ever since it was written. Jefferson may have meant only that white Americans in 1776 were equal with any other Englishmen, but words can be dangerous and, once they were written, America was committed to a great ideal.

When Abraham Lincoln quoted Jefferson in his Gettysburg address during the Civil War and stated this nation's dedication to the "proposition that all men are created equal," he was referring to the Negroes who would be free

35

men when the war ended. Lincoln, like almost every other white American of his day, probably did not feel that Negroes were his equal, but he did acknowledge the "proposition," or principle, that they were. With the Gettysburg address, Lincoln made equality the third war aim — after union and emancipation.[1] As we know, this aim, unlike the other two, was not achieved in his time.

If the abstraction of equality was as hard for Americans of the 1860's to get straight as it is for us, it is easy to see that grave practical problems faced the Negroes once freedom was theirs. How would they earn a living? Who would look after the people who were too old to work and the children without parents? The Reconstruction period was a time when Americans were forced to rebuild the social structure of the country in order to make a new accommodation for the Negroes living there.

In this section of our study, we will be looking at the Negroes living in the land of equality not as slaves but as freedmen. Our society first offered freedom to them and then turned its back as some of the nation's members curtailed or destroyed that freedom. Despite all disappointments, it was for America's black men a great revolutionary era full of fascinating experiences. They learned much, gained much, and lost much; for as one historian has noted speaking of this period, "revolutions may go backward."[2] By the end of the nineteenth century, the Civil War's bright promise of freedom was badly tarnished. The problems faced in this section raise the question of the meaning of equality in America; they ask who is responsible for giving that meaning substance.

---

[1] C. Vann Woodward, "Equality: The Deferred Commitment," *The Burden of Southern History* (Baton Rouge, 1960), pp. 69-87.

[2] Willie Lee Rose, *Rehearsal for Reconstruction: The Port Royal Experiment* (Indianapolis, 1964), p. 408, quoting Thomas Wentworth Higginson.

chapter 1

The Civil War Brings Freedom

Introduction

In the movies, the Civil War sometimes ends with the news of Appomattox reaching the old plantation. Saddened that his cause is lost but relieved that the faraway fighting is at last over, the master manfully goes out and tells his slaves that now they are free. The freedmen are pictured as joyful and the planter as hopeful that they will remain faithful workers in his fields. In fact, it sometimes happened much this way, but many of the 4 million Negroes of the South learned their first lessons about freedom in the chaos of the war itself. The conditions under which the ex-slaves began living as freedmen varied greatly.

How did the freed slaves respond to their new way of life? What, in turn, was the appropriate response for the government to make? These are the questions this chapter poses.

The Sea Island Experiment

Early in the war, when Union victories were scarce, the United States navy attacked the fortress on Hilton Head, an island in the Sea Island group off the coast of Charleston, South Carolina, and Savannah, Georgia. On these islands were large plantations on which was raised cotton of high quality. Planters' families came out from the mainland during the summer months to live in their fine houses and take advantage of the sea winds, but in normal times their stay was short and the Negro slaves lived an isolated life under the direction only of overseers.

On November 7, 1861, when Commodore Samuel Francis DuPont attacked, the planters who were in residence hurried to get away. Not all of them succeeded. The men who rowed one planter out to the federal ships were his own slaves, who improvised this song as they went along:

> De Norfmen dey's got massa now,
> De Norfmen dey's got massa now,
> De Norfmen dey's got massa now,
>   Hallelujah.

Oh! massa a rebel; we row him to prison.
  Hallelujah.
Massa no whip us any more.
  Hallelujah.
We have de Yankees, who no run away.
  Hallelujah.
Oh! all our old massas run away.
  Hallelujah.
Oh! massa going to prison now.
  Hallelujah.[1]

Other planters were luckier. Telling their slaves that the Yankees would sell them to Spanish slaveholders in Cuba or appealing to their loyalty, most of the white men were able to get enough hands to row them back to Charleston. But many Negroes, eager for freedom, remained behind and took their chances with the Yankees.

And chance it was. In a day, the discipline of slavery was gone. The ex-slaves were alone on their islands, sharing them only with a contingent of young Union soldiers from the distant North. The first reaction of some of the freedmen was to protest against the life they had been leading by burning the cotton gins. But in their destructiveness, the Negroes did not exceed the vigor of the Northern soldiers or the retreating planters, some of whom destroyed their harvested cotton on the theory that with the possession of cotton which still needed processing and handling, the slaves (as well as the cotton) would be an asset to the Union forces. Without the cotton, the ex-slaves, lacking jobs and subsistence, would be a liability to the Northern army.

When things quieted down, the Negroes began spending time around the army encampment as if missing the familiar authority of white men and wondering what the quality of the new masters would be. One Yankee soldier was bent on making the old massa's threats come true: he was caught attempting to round up a group of Negro fieldhands to make up a shipment of slaves for Cuba. These and other less drastic but prejudicial acts alarmed other white Northerners who hoped the Negroes would not be forced back into servitude.

Two Economic Systems

Northerners had two ideas about what should be done for the freedmen on the Sea Islands. One group attempted to follow the old plantation pattern, substituting wage labor for slave labor. This plan accommodated the Negro workers to a hard-headed Yankee business proposition. The Negroes' knowledge of the cotton crop was utilized and they lived as agricultural workers earning wages like factory workers in the North. The workers were safe from exploitation if the white superintendents sent from the North were humane men. When speculators, intent only on profits and

---

[1]Quoted in James M. McPherson, *The Negro's Civil War* (New York, 1965), p. 59.

unconcerned about the welfare of the freedmen, supervised the plantations, the Negroes were in for trouble. When the old masters returned after the war things got even worse.

Other Northerners hoped for a different system. A group of volunteers known as Gideon's Band came to the islands to conduct schools and help the freedmen begin their new way of life. These men and women, most of them young and all of them idealistic, were supported by the Freedmen's Aid Societies in the North, which had powerful members with important friends in Washington, such as Senator Charles Sumner of Massachusetts.

General Rufus Saxton was the man in charge of the freedmen's affairs on the Sea Islands. Laura Towne, one of the best schoolteachers in Gideon's Band, wrote in her diary: "General Saxton is much opposed to the sale of the land to speculators. He thinks they ought to be preempted [taken] by the people [the freedmen], or else divided and sold that the people can buy, and not be left a prey to greedy speculators and large landowners."[2] Largely through the tireless efforts of General Saxton, Miss Towne, and others who lobbied with President Lincoln and Secretary of War Stanton, not all of the lands were sold to speculators. Some were loaned to the freedmen, who worked the land, sold the cotton, and eventually bought the farms on which they were living.

The Fortunes of War

Few Negroes found the attaining of freedom as easy as the Sea Islanders did. Some of the bloodiest fighting of the Civil War took place along the Mississippi River in Mississippi and southwest Tennessee, and the slaves who lived there were caught between the two armies fighting back and forth across that ravaged corner of the South. Negroes were driven off plantations on which they had spent their entire lives by raiders who burned their houses. Often, the Negroes were shot either because, as laborers, they were able to bring in a cotton crop that would assist the enemy, or for no apparent reason at all.

As the Union Army was retreating to Memphis in the bitter cold of December, 1862, John Eaton, a chaplain, was put in charge of a group of Negro refugees who had been harrassed by Confederate forces. Eaton remembered that, in addition to the white troops who were crowded into the railroad cars, "each train carried crowds of contrabands* whom it was impossible either to organize or control. Their terror at being left behind made them swarm over the passenger and freight cars, clinging to every available space and even crowding the roofs. The trains moved very slowly . . . but even so the exposure of these people — men, women, and children — was indescribable."[3]

---

*A term for the ex-slaves, which denoted their first post-slavery role, that of seized property.

[2]Rupert Sargent Holland, ed., *Letters and Diary of Laura M. Towne* (Cambridge, 1912), p. 100.

[3]John Eaton, *Grant, Lincoln, and the Freedmen* (New York, 1907), p. 30.

After they reached Memphis, Eaton walked the snowy streets of the city and found that "at every corner little bonfires had been kindled around which shivering Negroes were huddled."[4] Eaton moved many of these Negroes into refugee camps which he ran under orders from General Grant. This provided rough care for some of the early arrivals, but the stream of refugees into Memphis did not stop. In July 1864, Eaton wrote to a friend describing the Negroes' conditions. Refugees were "crowded together, sickly, disheartened, dying on the streets, not a family of them all either well sheltered, clad or fed; no physicians, no medicines, no hospitals. . . . Such scenes . . . were calculated to make one doubt the policy of emancipation."[5]

Eaton was not hopeful about the possibility of finding a way that these 20,000 charges of his could make a living. Only twelve men cutting wood for river streamers were successfully self-employed and the "ideas" of the rest "had not been improved by idleness and association with the army. . . ."[6] As laborers, they came and went without regard for agreements they had made with employers (who, in any event, were most reluctant to pay them cash wages). Despite this, Eaton was not totally discouraged. He found the ex-slaves "not so far an exception to the rest of humanity as to be free from vice and crime," but he admired their courage making their way into the cities where he found them "an interesting and industrious class — manageable and susceptible of improvement." Eaton, an opponent of slavery and eager to raise money to assist the freedmen, concluded his letter with the statement that anyone "of a candid and unprejudiced mind cannot . . . fail to pronounce emancipation a success."

Broken in Spirit

Eaton's most trusted lieutenant, Samuel Thomas, a young businessman who was running some of the refugee camps in the country, was not so sure. In Memphis, the Negroes were huddled together in wire-enclosed clusters of huts and tents. They were protected, though not always successfully, from armed raiders who tried to take them back into slavery; their means of survival was to be rented out as gangs of laborers to raise cotton for Northern speculators who had leased confiscated cotton plantations along the Mississippi river. Early in the war Samuel Thomas wrote of one of these camps: "I hope I may never be called on again to witness the horrible scenes I saw in those first days of the history of the freedmen in the Mississippi Valley. . . . Our efforts to do anything for these people, as they herded together in masses, when founded on any expectation that they would help themselves, often failed; they had become so completely broken down in spirit, through suffering, that it was impossible to arouse them."[7]

---

[4]*Ibid.,* p. 31.
[5]*Ibid.,* p. 105.
[6]*Ibid.,* pp. 105-106.
[7]*Ibid.,* p. 19.

A Slave Takes a Chance

Sometimes individual Negroes, luckier in their environment, aroused themselves brilliantly to the opportunities freedom gave to them. Robert Smalls, for example, was a young man who had been brought up as a favored child in the house of his master in the pretty village capital of the Sea Islands, Beaufort. His mother had been brought from the plantation and made a house servant and Robert became the pet of his owner, Henry McKee.

When McKee went down to his plantation to supervise the distribution of food rations to the field hands, Smalls was sometimes taken along. The boy was troubled long before the Civil War by what he took to be the same lack of spirit on the part of the slaves that Samuel Thomas observed later in the Mississippi Valley. The people accepted the food apathetically with no observable emotion. They seemed to Smalls to be uninterested in asserting themselves in any way.

One day, however, McKee went back to Beaufort leaving Smalls behind on the plantation temporarily. Then, with the master gone, Robert heard the slaves grumble bitterly about the food they had been given. Far from not caring, the plantation Negroes proved deeply concerned about their condition. It was on this lonely spot, years before the Civil War, and not in the busier town of Beaufort, that Smalls first heard of the great Negro leader, Frederick Douglass, and determined to follow his example and seek his freedom.

Because he was in Charlestown at the time, Robert Smalls was not freed when the Union forces took the islands. He had been hired out by McKee and was the pilot of a coastal steamer, the *Planter,* which was engaged in carrying supplies and men to strengthen the Confederate defenses of Charleston. Smalls, however, was determined to escape and made his plans carefully. One night, when the white crew and officers were at a party on shore, Smalls quietly took the ship out into the harbor and went to another dock to pick up his wife and two children. Wearing the broad brim hat of *Planter's* white captain and maintaining a deceptive military stance, Smalls gave the appropriate signals to the Confederate soldiers in Fort Sumter and cleared the port. When Smalls and his crew came in sight of the Union gunboats off the islands, they raised a white bed sheet on the mast as a sign of truce and gave three cheers for the Union. Robert Smalls was a free man and soon was a hero throughout the North. During the rest of the war, he made daring raids into coastal rivers to pick up other escaping slaves and also built a lucrative business transporting Gideon's Band from island to island.[8]

His exploits were used by friends of emancipation to try to convince President Lincoln that slaves could make very enterprising free workers and excellent soldiers. Indeed, men and women like Rufus Saxton and Laura

[8]Dorothy Sterling, *Captain of the Planter: The Story of Robert Smalls* (New York, 1958), pp. 19, 30-34, 67-88.

Towne were deeply hopeful that their experiments with the former slaves on the Sea Islands would encourage just such enterprise among the freedmen. They contemplated that the program of assistance and encouragement for freedom established on the Sea Islands would be imitated all over the South once the war was won.

Hints of Trouble Accompany Victory

When General Sherman's March to the Sea was completed and Savannah taken, it appeared to the islanders that victory was near. But all of the fruits of victory did not prove sweet. Sherman's marauding troops treated many of the Negro refugees who followed them with great cruelty. And as soon as Savannah was taken, the white seccessionists, instead of cowering in defeat, began to assert once again their old prerogatives and talked of getting their island lands back. General Saxton and his wife came back from their first visit to Savannah and reported that: "Charities from the North are given to rank secesh* women, in silks, while poor whites & destitute negroes are turned away, and told to go to work."[9] As we will see, what the Saxtons observed in Savannah indicated what troubles the ex-slaves would have after the war.

Freedmen and the Government

Secretary of War Stanton also paid Savannah a visit in January 1865 and while there he invited twenty leaders of the Negro community to meet with him and advise on what the government's postwar freedmen policy should be. All but one of the Negroes in the delegation were natives of Georgia or South Carolina; the twentieth was a Methodist missionary from Maryland. Five of them were freeborn, three had bought their own freedom, three had been liberated by their masters, and nine had been freed by the war.

Garrison Frazier, a carpenter and part-time minister, spoke for the group. Diplomatically, he avoided being drawn into making accusations of anti-Negro acts by General Sherman, but instead said that freedom "as I understand it, promised by the proclamation, is taking us from under the yoke of bondage and placing us where we could reap the fruits of our own labor, take care of ourselves and assist the government in maintaining our freedom."[10] Asked whether they would prefer to have their farms scattered among the whites, or in colonies by themselves, Frazier replied that "we would prefer to live by ourselves for there is a prejudice against us in the South which will take years to get over." Only the Marylander dissented from this request for protective segregation.

Jubilee Day

Such sober assessments of both the promise and the problems of freedom were put aside when a delegation of Northern abolitionists came to Charles-

---

*An unfriendly nickname applied by Northerners to white Southern secessionists.
[9]Manuscript Diary of S. Willard Saxton, 24 January 1865, in private possession.
[10]*Official Records of the War of the Rebellion*, Series I, Vol. 47, part 2, pp. 37-41.

ton after the war to celebrate the raising of the Union flag over Fort Sumter. In the Negro Zion Church in Charleston, 3000 people came to salute the great abolitionist, William Lloyd Garrison, and the next day the most famous preacher of the time, Henry Ward Beecher, spoke in the same crowded auditorium on the blessings of victory and freedom. A "sprinkling of white officers & ladies" were in front "near the pulpit, the rest . . . [were] negroes of every size, sex, color, [and] age." As Beecher spoke, "emotion began to work in the audience like the rising of the wind in the forest or the sobbing of the waves upon the Beech." The men and their turbanned women in colorful plaid dresses were enthralled by Beecher as he extolled the glory of freedom. There were tears, there was laughter; and the sermon was even interrupted with the cry: "Thank you massa, Glory to God."[11]

A Sober Assessment

Enemies of slavery who did not think that praising freedom disposed of the problems facing the ex-slaves were made a little edgy by these great ceremonial occasions. From the Sea Islands, Rufus Saxton sent an invitation to Garrison, Beecher, and their party, which included a number of prominent newspapermen and several men important in public life, to come out to the islands to see how the freedmen were living on their new farms. The invitation was accepted, and the visitors were conducted on tours of the prospering plantations on which the Negroes worked as wage laborers.

Freedmen in school with Yankee schoolteachers.   *(The Bettmann Archive, Inc.)*

[11]Samuel Scoville to Harriet Beecher Scoville, 17 April 1865, Beecher Family Papers, Yale University.

As they drove along, the Northerners could also see farms worked by the luckier and more ambitious Negro farmers who had acquired their own.

Negro farmers neglected some of the tasks they had most hated as slaves, such as hauling up nitrogen-rich muck from the flats at low tide for use as fertilizer, but independently or in efforts in which resources and labor were pooled, the former slaves made use of the only trade slavery had taught them and became successful cotton growers. The practical "hoe and trowel" antislavery people who had been working with the freedmen on the islands for years knew that this solid economic base was essential to the well-being of the emancipated Negroes. And they knew that there was more to living than mere economics; the schools for the freedmen — children and adults — were the pride and joy of Gideon's Band.

On the Sunday that the Garrison-Beecher party was on the islands visiting sabbath schools, they received word that Lincoln had been shot. The nation was stunned and reminded that the recent end of the terrible Civil War was not the end of the country's problems. The new President, Andrew Johnson, would still have to make a major effort to reconstruct a nation so recently broken in two.

QUESTIONS

1. Account for the different attitude and spirit of Smalls and the Sea Island Negroes and those in southwest Tennessee described by Eaton and Thomas.

2. Based on the needs of the slaves as you understand them in this chapter and based on the treatment you expect they would get if abandoned to white Southerners, formulate a reconstruction policy for the freedmen.

SUGGESTED READING

Willie Lee Rose's *Rehearsal for Reconstruction: The Port Royal Experiment* (Indianapolis, 1964) is a fascinating study of the Negroes on the Sea Islands and of the efforts of Gideon's Band to direct their way to freedom. Benjamin Quarles' *The Negro in the Civil War* and Dudley Taylor Cornish's *The Sable Arm: Negro Troops in the Union Army, 1861-1865* (New York, 1966) discuss the participation of the Negroes in the war. James Mc-Pherson's *The Negro's Civil War* (New York, 1965) is a collection of documents relating to the same subject. Thomas Wentworth Higginson's *Army Life in a Black Regiment* (New York, 1962) tells of the experiences of a white abolitionist minister who was the colonel of a Negro regiment. It is one of the finest literary works to come out of the Civil War. Dorothy Sterling's *Captain of the Planter: The Story of Robert Smalls* (New York, 1958) is a lively biography for young readers which meets high standards of historical accuracy.

chapter 2
White Southerners Confront the Freedmen

Introduction

How the South would be reconstructed was the question confronting Andrew Johnson when he became President. No group had more at stake in the rebuilding of the nation than the freedmen and, as the war ended, there was much to make them optimistic. Before the fighting was over the Congress had passed and President Lincoln had signed a bill creating the Freedmen's Bureau, a federal agency designed to aid the ex-slaves. A victorious wartime commander, General O. O. Howard of Maine, who was known as the "Christian General," had been chosen to head the bureau. The freedmen appeared to have strong help available to them.

Many of the Negroes' Gideon's Band friends were also hopeful that the new President would prove zealous in the freedmen's cause. President Lincoln had never given up the hope that the Negroes might somehow be colonized outside the United States. On the other hand, as the wartime governor of Unionist Tennessee, Andrew Johnson had argued for strong Negro rights. After Lincoln's assassination, the freedmen looked to his successor to do even more for them than had the Great Emancipator, to whom they were so grateful.

In this they were disappointed; Andrew Johnson's radicalism did not survive the war. While the fighting raged, advocacy of Negro rights was a powerful weapon with which to threaten the enemy, the Confederate slave-owners. However, once the battles were over and peace was made at Appomattox, the President had to decide who should maintain order in the defeated South. The Congress was not in session and, after great victory parades, the rank and file of the army was swiftly mustered out of service. To Andrew Johnson it seemed logical that men experienced in governing the South should go on doing so; the job of reestablishing order belonged to white Southerners.

The purpose of this chapter is to examine Johnson's establishment of "home-rule," a program that denied lands to the freedmen in order to restore them to the white planters and allowed the passage of special laws regulating the freedmen's behavior.

Home Rule

On May 29, 1865, the President issued his Amnesty Proclamation with which he pardoned those Confederates who took the oath of allegiance and gave the others — rich and powerful members of the rebellious states — a chance to come to the White House and ask his forgiveness. This the President gave freely under the pardoning power granted to the chief executive by the Constitution. In return, Johnson expected the Southern leaders to cooperate with his program for restoration of peace and stability. The pardoned men were given back not only their political rights, but also lands taken from them during the war. In restoring these lands, the President was defying the Congress, which had said that the Freedmen's Bureau should use these lands to give some of the freedmen forty-acre farms of their own.[1]

Given political power so that they could restore order to their own region and ensure that war would not break out again, the white Southern leaders turned their first attention to reestablishing their authority over the Negroes. Discipline of the blacks had been the cornerstone of the social order during pre-war years and was considered all the more imperative now that the restraints of slavery no longer existed. The governments of the southern states, beginning in the summer of 1865, began drawing up new laws to define how the ex-slave Negroes were to live. These laws, which came to be known as the "Black Codes," have been the subject of heated controversy ever since.

Two Views of the Black Codes

Carl Schurz, a Union General who visited the South in the fall of 1865 as the Black Codes were being put into effect, felt that the defense of the codes rested on the same arguments which had been used to defend slavery: "It is that the negro exists for the special object of raising cotton, rice, and sugar *for the whites,* and that it is illegitimate for him to indulge, like other people, in the pursuit of his own happiness in his own way."[2]

Forty years later, William Dunning, a careful scholar who taught a whole generation of Reconstruction historians, regarded the codes as "conscientious attempts to bring some order out of social and emonomic chaos which a full scale acceptance of the results of war and emancipation involved." Dunning felt the "freedmen were not, and in the nature of the case could not be, on the same social, moral, and intellectual planes with the whites, and this fact was recognized by constituting them a separate class in the civil order."[3]

In order to assess whether Carl Schurz or William Dunning was more nearly correct in his evaluation of the Black Codes let us look at some of the provisions of the most stringent of these laws as enacted in Mississippi. In doing so, it might be well to bear in mind that they were passed to restore

---

[1]*United States Statutes at Large* XIII, pp. 507-509.
[2]Senate Executive Documents, No. 2, 39th Congress, 1st session, p. 21.
[3]William A. Dunning, *Reconstruction, Political and Economic, 1865-1877* (New York, 1907), p. 58.

(The Bettmann Archive, Inc.)

order to a region in which the Negroes had suffered heavily from the disorders of war (described earlier by John Eaton and Samuel Thomas). Moreover, it must finally be asked whether these codes were reasonable and beneficial to the Negroes in light of conditions at the time or whether they were, as General Schurz said, helpful only to Mississippi whites and a detriment to her black citizens.

Mississippi's Black Code

To the Mississippians who voted for "An Act to Confer Civil Rights on Freedmen," the provisions seemed essential to the restoration of order and economic prosperity to their state. The former slaves were awarded access to the courts. They could sue and they could be sued. They could also appear as witnesses in civil cases and in criminal cases where the victim of the crime was a black man. The former slaves were allowed to marry, and, though in separate ledgers, these marriages were recorded just as those of white couples were. The right of the Negroes to acquire and hold property of their own was also affirmed.

Although this legislation, with its promising title, conferred some rights that were denied the black people under slavery, it stated that the confirmation of the right to own property did not allow for the purchase or rental of lands outside of towns. The effect of this provision was to prevent ex-slaves from owning farmland; the dream of the freedmen of farming their own land, which the Congress tried to encourage, was thus denied them by state law.

Orphans under the Black Codes

In addition to establishing what the civil rights of the Negroes were to be and defining what their right to own property consisted of, the Mississippi legislature faced the problem of orphaned or destitute black children. The social and economic arrangements of slavery no longer covered these dependents. The solution arrived at by the Mississippi lawmakers permitted a judge to bind out Negro children to long-term apprenticeships without the consent of the children's parents if it was thought that the children would not be taken care of otherwise. This system of indentured labor was objected to by friends of the freedmen, who saw it as a resumption of slavery in another name. Its defenders pointed out that white children had long been bound out as apprentices. General Clinton Fisk, the head of the Freedmen's Bureau in Kentucky and Tennessee, had been bound out as a boy, as had Senator Henry Wilson of Massachusetts, and neither of them appeared harmed by the experience. Why, asked Southerners (who wondered who would care for the many Negro orphans in the South), should the Negroes be given favored treatment and not be bound out?

Vagrancy

The most fundamental justification for the Black Codes rested on the assumption that without the discipline of slavery the Negroes of the South would wander aimlessly about and create social disorder as well as neglect the staple crops of the region. If the economy was to be restored so that black men as well as white had enough to eat, it was essential that the Negroes go back to work on the plantations. The Mississippi Black Code met this problem as follows:

Sec. 5. Be it further enacted, that every freedman, free Negro and mulatto shall, on the second Monday of January, one thousand eight hundred and sixty-six, and annually thereafter, have a lawful home or employment, and shall have written evidence thereof, ...

Sec. 6. Be it further enacted, that all contracts for labor made with freedmen, free Negroes, and mulattoes . . . shall be in writing and . . . read to said freedman, free Negro, or mulatto, by . . . two disinterested white persons of the county in which the labor is to be performed. . . .

Sec. 7. Be it further enacted, that every civil officer shall, and every person may, arrest and carry back to his or her legal employer any freedman, free Negro, or mulatto who shall have quit the service of his or her employer before the expiration of his or her term of service without good cause; and said officer and a person shall be entitled to receive for arresting and carrying back every deserting employee aforesaid the sum of five dollars, and ten cents per mile from the place of arrest to the place of delivery; and the same shall be paid by the employer, and held as a set-off for so much against the wages of said deserting employee. . . .

Sec. 9. Be it further enacted, that if any person shall persuade or attempt to persuade, entice, or cause any freedman, free Negro, or mulatto to desert from the legal employment . . . he or she shall be guilty of misdemeanor. . . .[5]

---

[4]Vernon Lane Wharton, *The Negro in Mississippi, 1865-1890* (New York, 1965), p. 89.

[5]*Ibid.*, pp. 83-85.

In a nutshell, what the Mississippi legislators, like other lawmakers across the South, seemed to be saying was that they would tolerate no vagrancy on the part of the Negroes. In 19th-century America, which put a high premium on industrious work habits, the toleration of indolent drifters was not to be expected. Most observers of the Black Codes, like William Dunning, thought the legislators reasonable men. But even at the time not all Americans reacted that way when they realized how laws like this could affect the freedmen.

The Case of John Martin

In July, 1865, a shabbily dressed, country Negro named John Martin was walking along a New Orleans street with a crate of chickens in his hand. He was stopped by a city policeman and arrested for vagrancy under a city ordinance similar to the one in neighboring Mississippi. A magistrate doubted Martin's word that the chickens belonged to him and sentenced him to six months in the workhouse. It was commonly understood that Negroes so sentenced could escape the workhouse by signing a contract to work on the sugar plantations, which were suffering from a labor shortage.

Since the United States purchased Louisiana from France, there had been a sizable population of free middle-class Negroes in New Orleans, but the end of slavery and the harsh work conditions on the sugar plantations brought more and more ex-slave farm workers into town. Perhaps, it was not idleness but ambition which made an enterprising young man like John Martin come to the city to try to sell his chickens. The Negro newspaper, *The New Orleans Tribune,* protested the arrest of John Martin, and so did Thomas Conway, an assistant commissioner of the Freedmen's Bureau in New Orleans.

"What right had he [the policeman] to make the arrest?" Conway asked in a letter to the mayor of New Orleans. "None whatsoever," he declared, answering his own inquiry, "except that it is right to arrest as vagrants all who are poorly dressed, or may be found carrying chickens . . . along the streets. But the trouble was not that John was poorly dressed or that he carried chickens that he raised from the hour that they came from the shell, but that he was black."[6]

The President's Response

Conway's letter did not help John Martin. Mayor Kennedy regarded it as an example of unwarranted Northern interference in the governing of his city. He sent the letter to President Johnson as a sample of the meddling ways of the Freedmen's Bureau. The President sympathized fully with the mayor's position. Before the year's end, Thomas Conway had been relieved of his post in the Freedmen's Bureau by a man who cooperated fully with the New Orleans police. In addition, the commissioner of the bureau, General Howard, was sent on a tour across the South to reassure white

---

[6]Thomas Conway to Hugh Kennedy, 13 July 1865, Andrew Johnson Papers, Library of Congress microfilm.

Southerners, who were reestablishing their positions of dominance in their states, that the agents of the Freedmen's Bureau could be counted on to encourage the ex-slaves to continue working for their former masters. The ex-slaves would not be encouraged to leave the field gangs to raise and market chickens, as John Martin had done. To members of Gideon's Band it was obvious that the "secesh in silks" were quickly getting their way.

Land Restoration

While he was in Charleston, South Carolina, General Howard engaged Robert Smalls (who had bought the *Planter* from the United States government) to take him out to the Sea Islands. The President had sent Howard to convince the freedmen of Edisto Island to yield their farms and also not to leave the islands and deprive the returning white planters of a needed labor force. Pardoned white planters had been returned their plantations by President Johnson and the Negroes were told they had to leave the farms which had been theirs since the planters abandoned them during the war. When the general and his three white companions arrived, the black men of Edisto organized their resistance. Howard remembered a triumphant visit to the Sea Islands the previous January and the visits he paid to charming Sunday Schools run by sympathetic Northern white men and women. Now Edisto seemed a foreign land. The Edisto farmers were menacing: "their eyes flashed unpleasantly." Howard noticed "one very black man, thickset and strong" who denounced the general with great power. Howard could not even get enough quiet to make his talk until a Negro woman, in a corruption of religion, silenced the black protest, by starting to sing the hymn, 'Nobody knows the trouble I feel — nobody knows but Jesus.'

Then Howard could speak. His tone was that of a man of reason speaking to reasonable men, but he found the Negroes did not consider giving up their lands reasonable. Repeatedly, they said they wanted to buy the lands out of their crop earnings — to gain the lands out of the proceeds of their labor on them. To this argument Howard said, "Congress must meet, before any public lands can be had and before I can buy any for you."[7]

His promise was a thin one. There was little assurance that the farmers would get to keep their lands. Howard had done his duty to the President by going to Edisto, but he hurried back to Charleston "before dark after rather a hard and sad day's work."[8] As Howard continued his trip across the South, he continued to learn how saddened the freedmen were at the way freedom was running. In Mobile, 600 Negro school children were to have their promising beginning in education ended so that the buildings could be given back to the white medical school. In New Orleans, he heard Negro leaders complain about the restoration of lands to the Confederate owners, the attempts to halt the Negro's efforts to get the vote, and Thomas Con-

---

[7] Oliver Otis Howard, *Autobiography of Oliver Otis Howard* (2 vols., New York, 1908), *2*, pp. 235-237.
[8] Manuscript diary of S. Willard Saxton, 19 Oct. 1865.

way's successor in the Freedmen's Bureau in that city, James Scott Fullerton, who was actively assisting in rounding up "vagrants."

The New Orleans Tribune spoke the bitterness of the freedmen all over the South when it published a letter from Frederick Douglass, who borrowed the old language of slavery to say of the President, "Johnson has sold us."[9] The Negroes were forced to look to Congress to protect them from what many of them thought to be a substitution for slavery imposed by white Southerners with their Black Codes.

QUESTIONS

1. Do you agree with the basic assumption behind the Mississippi Black Codes that some special laws had to be passed to regulate the behavior of the freedman, or do you think the freedman was ready for and should have been given the same rights as whites?

2. What does John Martin's case tell us about the way the "vagrancy" principle of the Black Codes was applied? Based on the case, do you agree with Shurtz's or Dunning's interpretation of the code? Why?

3. Do you agree with President Andrew Johnson's decision to turn the keeping of order over to white Southerners?

SUGGESTED READING

An excellent addition to the growing list of state studies which are sensitive to the Negroes' post-war aspirations is Joel Williamson's *After Slavery: The Negro in South Carolina During Reconstruction, 1861-1877* (Chapel Hill, 1965). It builds on the tradition established by the pioneering, white Southern scholar Vernon Lane Wharton, whose work *The Negro in Mississippi, 1865-1890* (New York, 1965) is now available in paperback.

---

[9]Frederick Douglass to J. B. Roudanez, quoted in *New Orleans Tribune*, 27 Oct., 1865.

chapter 3
The Congress Responds

Introduction

During the spring and summer of 1865, President Andrew Johnson had free rein in carrying out a reconstruction policy which turned the job of keeping law and order in the South to white Southerners. Congress met again in December 1865, amidst many misgivings about the direction that Johnson's policies were taking the Union, the freedmen, and the Republican party. One of their misgivings was that repression of Negroes would be so severe that they would engage in acts of insurrection. Certainly, reports from the South gave a dismal picture of the Negro's treatment by his former master; stories of killings, lynchings, and other acts of repression abounded. Consequently, Congress set out to investigate the conditions in the South, particularly the treatment of the freedman. While this investigation was under way, during May 1866, bloody fighting broke out on the streets of Memphis and lasted for three days. Shortly after the disturbances ended, a special three-man Congressional investigating committee was sent to Tennessee to determine the cause of the riot and the steps Congress might take to prevent similar outbursts. Much of the testimony was conflicting, and the committee was forced to choose between different versions of the same incident. Some of the testimony before the committee follows, large parts of it as much a reflection of the social outlook of a particular witness as an account of what he saw.

How the Riot Started

One view of the riot presented to the committee was that of Dr. S. J. Quimby, a Memphis physician. Dr. Quimby testified that on Tuesday afternoon, May 1, some hundred colored troops were "out on a drunk" awaiting their pay. Dr. Quimby reported that when the police arrested two disorderly Negro soldiers, the fight began.

> . . . I heard firing; on looking over towards Main street I saw about one hundred and fifty colored soldiers; they were chasing officers in all directions; they chased two right down by me; there were about six men after the two;

52

they were calling out to the policemen, "Halt," and firing after them all the time. There were at least fourteen shots fired at one of the officers. As they came down into Shelby street I saw a black man come up, armed with a Spencer rifle, who called out to the officers, "Halt, you white son of a bitch," and fired at him. The officer kept on; this was about dark; the soldiers went at once into the fort and were not out during the night again. About ten o'clock at night there came up into the street about two hundred men, policemen and posse; they came and patrolled up and down the streets, but found nobody or any force to oppose them. Then they broke up into small squads and went among the colored people's houses.[1]

Troops Denied

The committee knew that when these squads left the neighborhood, many of the residents were dead and many houses burned. The investigators wondered about the ability and willingness of the local authorities both to maintain order and also to protect the blacks, and thus solicited the testimony of both military and civilian officials. Major General George Stoneman testified that the local sheriff had asked for federal troops to quell the riot and that, in the interest of seeing whether the local citizenry were able to provide for themselves, he had witheld such troops. Furthermore, stated the General, he had told the sheriff that he would give arms only to responsible parties who he felt would obey military authorities; the men the sheriff brought — "some of [whom] were firemen, some discharged Confederate soldiers, some of them [not belonging] to anything except the rabble of the town . . ." — the General felt were not proper men to be trusted with arms.[2]

Mr. Winters, the sheriff of Memphis, also was called before the committee. He reported his request to General Stoneman for troops and then went on:

> He told me he had no soldiers to give me; that the people here had petitioned the government to have the troops removed, and I had to go and summon my *posse.* . . . It was then about dusk. . . . There was then a great crowd of men, women and children on the sidewalk, and there was, I expect, about half a dozen shots fired. I got out of the way myself. I didn't know but I might get shot. . . . I met six soldiers, two or three of whom had guns, and one appeared to be an orderly. They told me they came from General Stoneman's headquarters, and commenced taking pistols from the few men I had in charge with me. I begged them not to take the pistols away. . . . I saw very few police. I took with me my own *posse.* This was on the first day.

Rumor and Investigation

> The next day, [Wednesday] about nine o'clock, I was in my office, when word came up that the negroes had come out of the fort and were killing everybody. Judge Leonard ordered me to go and summon a *posse* of five hundred men. . . . I then went down to South street. When I got there a very large crowd had assembled. The first thing I saw was two white men, one a policeman and the other a citizen, taking a negro dressed in federal uniform towards the crowd. I got ahead of the crowd and told them not to interfere with the negro; that I came down there to protect black and white; that I was there as an officer of the peace, and would arrest any man who made disturbance. I took the negro, I expect, about fifty yards and put him in his

---

[1]39th Congress, 1st Session, *House of Representatives Report,* No. 101, "Memphis Riots and Massacres," (serial #1274) p. 104.
[2]*Ibid.,* pp. 50-51.

cabin. . . . I dispersed the crowd at that point and went on as far as the Hernando road, where I found another crowd. They had four negroes in the middle of them, and one of the negroes was being beat. I rode up as quick as I could and told them not to hurt the negroes. I sent two of my *posse* with the four negroes to the edge of the wood the other side of the Hernando road with orders to there turn them loose, which I waited to see them do. I expect those negroes did not stop running till night. If I had not been there I expect they would have been killed by a parcel of lawless white men who were prowling round there to burn up everybody's house, to rob and steal. . . .[3]

Sheriff Winters concluded his testimony with the remark that, insofar as he was aware, the only arrest made in connection with the riots was that of a nondescript, wounded Negro.

(The Bettmann Archive, Inc.)

Also considered by the committee was the statement of Martin T. Ryder, a United States marshal living in Memphis. In part, Ryder reported as follows:

[3] *Ibid.,* pp. 80-83.

The first thing I saw was a negro man running along the street and fifty or sixty men after him with pistols, some firing at him. The negro was not armed, but scared to death. I noticed that there were two or three policemen in the crowd, and I ordered them not to fire, but to take him. Going further, I found a policeman going toward the city, and I asked him if the difficulty was all over. He said it was not; that the negroes were all armed with guns, and that they could not fight them with pistols, but were going back to get guns. I continued my ride to where they said the disturbance had been, but found everything quiet, there was no disturbance whatever. I found one or two negroes lying dead on the street, and the negro people were afraid to go out and take them away. I stopped and spoke to some of them, and told them to take the men in . . . a man came up to me and asked what I was doing there. I said I was an officer trying to keep the peace. He said, "I know who you are." He had a pistol in his hand. He called me an abolitionist, and said . . . I was "worse than a nigger." He struck me on the head and tried to knock me down, and I expected every moment to lose my life. I had a pistol on, but had not an opportunity to use it. . . . Soon after I met the editor of the *Argus,* and I stated the facts to him. He told me the city was in a very dangerous condition; that, as a United States officer, I should see General Stoneman and tell him that the city was in danger of being destroyed; that the mob had full sway, and that innocent lives were being taken. I said, "Where is the mayor?" He said, "The mayor is intoxicated." [4]

"Keeping Law and Order"

Of no less interest to the committee were the opinions of the residents of Memphis themselves. One Alexander Mitcheler testified that he heard John Creighton, Memphis city recorder, addressing a crowd of white men. Creighton said, "Boys, I want you to go ahead and kill the last damned one of the nigger race, and burn up the cradle . . . God damn them. They are free, free indeed, but God damn them, we will kill and drive the last one of them out of the city." Mitcheler said the men drove him away before he could hear Creighton finish his speech.[5]

Another Memphis resident, John T. Oldbridge, testified about the actions of one O'Hearn, a Memphis constable and member of the sheriff's posse. Oldbridge testified that on the night of Wednesday, May 2:

> I saw O'Hearn call off three or four of the party, and, after some consultation in the street, he went with two others to the northeast corner of that negro school-house. I saw him pile up some matter and strike a match . . . the whole building was soon in flames . . . a policeman . . . named John Mickey, had on a federal overcoat and had a revolver in his hand. I heard him say, "May the mon that sit that on fire niver be sick . . ." I heard them say they were going to burn "every nigger building, every nigger church, and every God damn son of a bitch that taught a nigger.[6]

Still another Memphis resident, John E. Moller, testified about the violent actions of the city's law enforcement officials. Moller spoke of the shooting of an innocent Negro at the hands of a policeman and a fireman. He was then asked about additional acts of violence to which he had been a witness. Moller replied "I saw them knock down a little negro boy just on

---

[4]*Ibid.,* pp. 252-253.
[5]*Ibid.,* p. 355.
[6]*Ibid.,* p. 123.

the opposite side of the street . . . there was a policeman on horseback —
a lieutenant, or sergeant, or whatever he was; he said 'Kill them all together.'
. . . [The boy] did not do anything but cry. He hallooed to them to let him
alone . . . [but they said] that the God d—d niggers ought to be killed all
together — no matter — the small and the big ones."[7]

(The Bettmann Archive, Inc.)

The Negro Testimony

Possibly even more significant to the committee was the testimony of the
Negroes themselves. Not unusual were the statements of one of them, Mrs.
Sarah Long. She was asked what she had seen of the rioting, and responded:

> I saw them kill my husband . . . there were between twenty and thirty men
> who came to the house; when they first came, they hallooed to us to open the
> doors; my husband was sick in bed and could not get up; he had been sick in
> bed two weeks; he had the jaundice; I lay there, I was so scared; we have two
> children who were with us. They broke the outside doors open; I staid in the
> bed till they came in; the inside door was open; they came into the room and
> asked if we had any pistols or shot guns in the house; my husband said he had
> one, but it was only a rusty pistol, that his little boy had found; it was fit for
> nothing but the child to play with; then they told my husband to get up and

[7]*Ibid.*, p. 87.

get it; he got up and gave it to them. I then lighted a lamp after they got the pistol; they told my husband to get up and come out, that they were going to shoot him; they made him get up and go out of doors; he told them he was very sick; they said they did not care a damn; they took him out of doors and told him if he had anything to say, to say it quick, for they were going to kill him . . . they asked him if he had been a soldier; he said he never had been. One of them said, "You are a damned liar; you have been in the government service for the last twelve or fourteen months." "Yes," said he, "I have been in the government service, but not as a soldier." Then another said, "Why did you not tell us that at first?" Then one stepped back and shot him as quick as he said that; he was not a yard from him; he put the pistol to his head and shot him three times . . . when my husband fell he scuffled about a little, and looked as if he tried to get back into the house; then they told him that if he did not make haste and die, they would shoot him again. Then one of them kicked him, and another shot him again when he was down; they shot him through the head every time, as far as I could see. He never spoke after he fell.[8]

The Effects of the Riot

The committee heard too from General Benjamin P. Runkle, superintendent of the Freedmen's Bureau for the district of Memphis. He began with a description of his prior relationship with the freedmen:

I have always counselled them that liberty meant the right to work for themselves, to get their own living, and live honestly as white people do; I have always counselled them that they had no right to put themselves on an equality with white people, nor to presume to do anything of the kind; whenever they have made contracts, I have told them, and instructed my officers to tell them, that they must fulfill their contracts; that they must always at least work ten hours a day, and, under certain circumstances, more than that; that they must be obedient to their employers, and peaceable; that on the other hand their employers were bound to treat them well; to furnish them with healthy rations and good quarters, and I would see that their employers paid them; but that it was also my business to see that they performed their contracts.

Asked about the effect of the riot on the Negroes, General Runkle could only sadly reply, "It has put them back further than they were when I began; they have lost all confidence, I may say, in everything; they will not heed my counsel; when they come to see me they say, 'You are the man we expected to protect us;' I had no troops and could not do anything, and they have had very little confidence in me or in the government since that [time]; I have been doing what little I could to restore it, but I have not succeeded as well as I hoped to have done."[9]

In its final report, the committee concluded that the riots resulted in damage to private property of $116,000, damage to public property of $17,000, the known deaths of two whites and forty-six Negroes. What was to prove more important, however, was the way in which the committee members themselves were to respond in voting on Reconstruction measures.

To Congressman Shanklin of Kentucky, the investigation proved that efforts must be made to give what he considered a "more intelligent and a

---

[8]*Ibid.*, p. 222.
[9]*Ibid.*, p. 276.

better portion of society in the State" full control of reconstruction.[10] But the testimony indicated to the other men on the special investigating committee that the well-being of the Negro could not be trusted to Southern whites and that the federal government must assert its authority in the South. This conclusion was shared by the Republican Congress and much of the North.

The Fourteenth Amendment

In the Spring of 1866, even before the riot, Congress framed and sent to the states for their ratification, the 14th Amendment to the Constitution. The first critical section of the amendment made Negroes citizens of the United States and denied states the power to take away their rights:

> All persons born or naturalized in the United States, and subject to the jurisdiction thereof, are citizens of the United States and of the State wherein they reside. No State shall make or enforce any law which shall abridge the privileges or immunities of citizens of the United States; nor shall any State deprive any person of life, liberty, or property, without due process of law; nor deny to any person within its jurisdiction the equal protection of the laws.

The wording of this amendment was vague as generations of students and judges who have tried to decipher its meaning have discovered to their dismay. Later chapters deal with some of the twists and turns in the interpretations of the 14th Amendment engineered by the Supreme Court in the one hundred odd years since its passage. Congressmen failed to spell out clearly the meaning of this amendment because they were concerned with Negroes who lived in the South, and Constitutional amendments apply to the country as a whole. Northern voters were not ready to give the Negro next door equality as Connecticut's electorate proved, refusing to enfranchise Negroes in April, 1865. The 14th Amendment therefore became a vague and abstract doctrine, but it did for the first time bring the word *equal,* used in the Declaration of Independence, into the Constitution itself, and it prohibited the States from depriving citizens of their Constitutional right to equality.

The Military Reconstruction Acts

A prerequisite to the South's admission into the Union set forth by the Congress was that the states ratify the 14th Amendment. When Southern states failed to ratify the amendment, Congress enacted the first of the military Reconstruction acts, dividing the South into five military districts, and ordered the military (including the Freedmen's Bureau agents who were now under the direction of the military commanders) to register the Negroes to vote. White men who had served the Confederacy were disenfranchised and white Unionists and Negroes were empowered to draw up new state constitutions and stand for election to the state officerships and legislatures. "Black Reconstruction," the era of the rule of the South by the "Carpetbag-

---

[10]*Ibid.,* pp. 37-44.

gers" (white Northerners living in the South), "scalawags" (white Southerners who were not disenfranchised and chose to participate in politics), and
Negroes, began. The next two chapters tell the story of these governments
and of the way white supremacy was re-established in the South.

QUESTIONS

1. Are there any differences between Dr. Quimby's account of the riot
and the accounts of other Memphis citizens? If so, how do you account for
them?
2. Did Black Codes and the Memphis riot prove that the federal government must protect Negroes?
3. When framing the 14th Amendment Congress made the Negro a citizen
of the United States as well as of his state and thereby opened the door
to the question what that citizenship means. What should this citizenship
mean?

SUGGESTED READING

There are no secondary accounts which do justice to the disturbances
in Memphis, New Orleans, and elsewhere in the South in 1866. The
standard work on the 14th Amendment is Joseph B. James' *The Framing
of the Fourteenth Amendment* (Urbana, 1956).

chapter 4
Radical Reconstruction

Introduction

The Reconstruction Era is, perhaps, the most controversial period in our past. During debates in Congress in our own time, senators advocating more civil rights for America's Negroes studiously avoid mention of Reconstruction days, while Southern opponents of such legislation try as hard as possible to make people think that it will cause a return to the evils of that period. Why is it that friends of the Negro today should want to avoid pointing to the time in our history when many Negroes held posts of great importance in the governments of the Southern states? It is because the picture drawn has been most unflattering to the Negroes of America. It is commonly believed that while black men were active in the governing of the South, the region lay prostrate.

The post-Civil War Congress, alarmed by such events as the Memphis riots and troubled conditions in the South under Reconstruction favored by President Johnson, turned the governing of the South over to a new electorate of Southerners, one that included Negroes. Some former Confederates were disenfranchised; still more chose to stay out of politics rather than share the legislative halls with black men. In no state, save South Carolina, were the Negroes ever in the majority in either house of the legislature and in none was there a Negro governor. Nevertheless, this period of Negro political activity in the South is known as "Black Reconstruction" or "Radical Reconstruction." And ever since that period, from 1867 to 1877, the performance of the Negro has been pointed to as proof that he should not be trusted to govern.

In this chapter, two pictures of Radical Reconstruction will be shown. One is drawn by a white abolitionist from Maine, James S. Pike, whose portrait of the South Carolina Negroes as lawmakers has dominated the nation's view of Black or Radical Reconstruction ever since. The second picture will draw on the story of Robert Smalls, the slave who had piloted the steamer *Planter* past the guns of Fort Sumter. Smalls was a leading politician during Reconstruction.

60

As you look at these two views of the Negro in the governing of the South during Reconstruction, ask yourself which is the more accurate. If you are satisfied that Robert Smalls as an active politician is more believable than Robert Smalls as a "ring-tailed baboon," ask yourself why, until our own time, almost all white Americans have chosen Pike's view of Reconstruction. Did the Negro prove himself unfit to govern?

James S. Pike, Abolitionist

Abolitionists like James S. Pike worked hard to convince their fellow Americans that slavery was a disgrace to the nation. When the soldiers had fought the Civil War and the abolitionists' work was done, Pike was one of the antislavery men who was not prepared for what came in Reconstruction. Anxious to rid America of slaves, the abolitionists discovered that when the "peculiar institution" was ended, the black slaves were still black and were still present in the society. And, in Radical Reconstruction, many of the ex-slaves proved that they took freedom seriously and were anxious to participate fully in all the activities which free white men enjoyed. This included making the laws by which they were governed.

In 1873, Pike, who had long been a reporter for the New York *Tribune,* visited the legislature in Columbia, South Carolina, and wrote an account of what he saw.

"The Dusky Tide"

"Yesterday, about 4 PM," wrote Pike, "the assembled wisdom of the State . . . issued forth from the State-House. About three-quarters of the crowd belonged to the African race. They were of every hue, from the light octoroon to the deep black. They were such a looking body of men as might pour out of a market-place or a court-house at random in any Southern State. Every negro type and physiognomy was here to be seen from the genteel serving-man to the rough-hewn customer from the rice or cotton field. . . . The dusky tide flowed out into the littered and barren grounds. . . . These were the legislators of South Carolina."[1]

Pike offers his judgement early on. "In the place of [the] old aristocratic society stands the rude form of the most ignorant democracy that mankind ever saw, invested with the functions of government. . . . It is barbarism overwhelming civilization by physical force. It is the slave rioting in the halls of his master, and putting the master under his feet. And, though done without malice and without vengeance, it is nevertheless . . . absolutely done. Let us," invited Pike, "approach nearer and take a closer view. We will enter the House of Representatives. Here sit one hundred and twenty-four members. Of these, twenty-three are white men, representing the old civilization. These are good-looking, substantial citizens . . . from the hill country. . . . There they sit, grim and silent. . . . They stolidly survey the noisy riot that goes on in the great Left and Centre."

---

[1]James S. Pike, *The Prostrate State: South Carolina Under Negro Government* (New York, 1935), p. 10.

"One of the things that first strike a casual observer in this negro assembly is the fluency of debate, if the endless chatter that goes on there can be dignified with this term. The leading topics of discussion are all well understood by the members, as they are of a practical character, and appeal directly to the personal interests of every legislator, as well as to his constituents. When an appropriation bill is up to raise money to catch and punish the Ku-klux, they know exactly what it means. They feel it in their bones. So, too, with educational measures. The free school comes right home to them; then the business of arming and drilling the black militia. They are eager on this point. Sambo can talk on these topics . . . day in and day out."[2]

These topics were important but, nevertheless, Pike was troubled. He wrote that it was "a Black Parliament . . . the only one on . . . earth which is the representative of a white constituency . . . The Speaker is black, the Clerk is black, the door-keepers are black, the little pages are black, the chairman of Ways and Means is black, and the chaplain is coal-black."[3]

Pike was not alone in being dismayed at the appearance of the Negroes in South Carolina legislative halls. A Northern Baptist minister and schoolman, Basil Manly, Jr., wrote in 1870:

One view of Negro legislators.   *(The Bettmann Archive, Inc.)*

---

[2]*Ibid.*, pp. 12-17.
[3]*Ibid.*, p. 15.

"The entrance halls both upstairs and down were thronged with negroes, who were keeping up a sort of saturnalia, haw-hawing, buying and selling peanuts, candy and gumgers, two or three walking arm in arm with noisy demonstrations, one party wrestling, another tugging at each other's coattails in play, somewhat after the manner of the game of 'last tag'. . . . an uproar was kept up, which ascended through the building into the open door of the Legislative halls, and did not facilitate hearing what was going on there."[4]

Corruption and Perspective

To make themselves fully at ease, the legislators spent a good deal of money refurbishing the State House. Eighteen hundred dollars were spent on cuspidors, handsomely decorated and stamped "House of Representatives"; six marble clocks were bought from Belgium for $885; five gilt mirrors cost $2137; while for $960 the speaker's chamber was graced with an even more handsome mirror decorated with shield, eagle, and the State symbol, a palmetto.[5] But it was not these extravagances alone which troubled Pike and many other historians who have looked at the Reconstruction legislature in South Carolina. More important was the unethical appropriation of state funds by members of the legislature. In the legislative year 1871-72, $1,533,574 were spent on salaries and other legislative expenses in comparison to $84,096 spent under a reform administration in 1876-77.[6] One of many ways this money got into the pockets of legislators and their friends was the "printing ring" in which newspaper printing plants owned by men in the government charged exorbitant prices for printing the bills passed by the legislature. There were also numerous scandals involving favors voted the railroads in return for which the legislators were enabled to make profits in the stock in the railroad company. Pike's judgement was that the legislators "stole right hand and left with a recklessness and audacity without parallel."

That unethical and illegal acts were committed by the black and white legislature of Reconstruction South Carolina is documented past argument. And similar corruption existed in other states in the South where the Negroes were not in a majority in the legislature. One historian of Reconstruction, J. G. de Roulac Hamilton, speaking of North Carolina, blamed this on the presence of Negroes in politics who were responsible for the "blunting of the moral sense of the white people."[7] Another historian, while not contending that two wrongs make a right, points out that during this same era "Boss" William M. Tweed's group in New York "took more than $100,000,000 from the city."[8] This sum dwarfed the thefts in South Carolina. This was the time of graft practiced by members of President Grant's cabinet, and Reconstruction historian John Hope Franklin speaking

---

[4]Basil Manly, Jr., quoted in Joel Williamson, *After Slavery* (Chapel Hill, 1965), p. 380.
[5]Francis Butler Simkins and Robert Hilliard Woody, *South Carolina During Reconstruction* (Chapel Hill, 1952), p. 130.
[6]*Ibid.*, p. 139.
[7]J. G. de Roulac Hamilton quoted in John Hope Franklin, *Reconstruction After the Civil War* (Chicago, 1961), p. 146.
[8]Franklin, *Reconstruction After the Civil War,* p. 147.

A second view of black politicians. *(The Bettmann Archive, Inc.)*

of the corruption in the black Reconstruction governments in the Southern states concludes that it "was only part of a national tragedy."[9]

But was all of Black Reconstruction a tragedy? The acts of corruption were, but not all the things that these legislatures did was harmful to their states. The Constitution of South Carolina, drawn up by the Convention of 1868, which had a black majority, was so ably constructed that it was not changed when Reconstruction ended. (It was amended only in 1895 when white supremacists changed it in order to deny the Negroes the vote.) When Martha Schofield, the Quaker teacher, visited the South Carolina legislature, the debate was not about the purchase of spitoons but about the desirability of a bill outlawing capital punishment. The record for progressive legislation during Reconstruction is commended even by historians who see the period as a tragic one for the South.

Negro Legislators

And who was the Negro who was in politics during Black Reconstruction? Pike called him "Sambo" and many writers since have spoken of him as if he were only part of a group — the "black majority" or the "colored bloc."[10] Like any other members of a legislative body, there were individuals, some good, some bad, and all different.

---

[9]*Ibid.*, p. 15.
[10]Pike, *The Prostrate State*, p. 17.

On the state level, there were men like Francis L. Cardozo who, as Treasurer of South Carolina, is credited with resisting many attempts at fraud. He was reportedly the son of a Jewish scholar of Charleston and a Negro mother. He was educated for the clergy in Edinburgh, Scotland, and later was minister of a Negro church in New Haven, Connecticut. After his years in politics in South Carolina, he served on the faculty of Howard University in Washington, D.C.

Mississippi sent the first Negro, Hiram Revels, to the United States Senate in 1870 and later elected Blanche K. Bruce as its second black Senator. South Carolina sent the most Negroes to Congress — six in all — and it was not until 1901 that the last of the Southern Negro Congressmen lost his seat in the House of Representatives. Not one of these legislators achieved great power in the Congress but neither were they nonentities. Hiram Revels is remembered more for his dignity and for the symbolic quality of serving in the Senate from Mississippi, than for any political leadership. Blanche Bruce, however, was a skillful politician who interested himself in foreign affairs while in the Senate. And in South Carolina, Robert Smalls was one of the political leaders of his state.

Robert Smalls in Politics

Robert Smalls had become so successful a businessman operating *The Planter* that he had been able to buy his former master's house in Beaufort.[11] In the fall of 1867, under the Congressional Reconstruction acts, Robert Smalls was appointed a registrar of voters in his native St. Helena Parish.* Negroes were registered and, being in a heavy majority on the Sea Islands, gave a commanding vote in favor of a new constitution. Some white voters who had been rebels were not allowed to vote; others did not choose to share balloting with Negroes. The vote across the state was in favor of a new constitution and Robert Smalls was elected a delegate to the convention which was to meet in Charleston to draft it.

The Charleston Convention

Robert Smalls and the other delegates were greeted with great hostility by many white Charlestonians, and there were crowds at the door of the clubhouse where the meeting was to take place. Smalls had to push his way into the building. A majority of the delegates were Negroes. Some of them were field hands visiting the city for the first time and could neither read nor write. Others, like Robert Smalls, had learned to read since the war and were successful businessmen. Others had been free Negroes and literate for many years. More than half of the white delegates were native South Carolinians; — some of them were from the up-country, which had never before been able to challenge the political power of the aristocratic

---

[11]The entire account of Robert Smalls and the quotations are taken from Sterling, *Captain of the Planter,* Chapters 19-24.
*South Carolina gave the name parish to what we would today call counties or assembly districts.

planters of the low country. Among the white delegates from the North were members of Gideon's Band, who had already demonstrated their friendship for the Negroes.

White opponents of Negroes in politics tried to ridicule the convention by calling it a "circus" of "black baboons" and "ring-tailed monkeys." When the convention came to order, however, the delegates proved to be intensely serious about the business at hand and somberly attentive to the tedious niceties of parliamentary procedure. They voted not to hire a chaplain in order to save the state money, and they also economized by not hiring extra clerks, messengers, and doorkeepers. As one delegate put it, "Most of us have been used to waiting on ourselves and I think we can do it yet."

The Negro delegates did not use their power to balance up the debts of slavery oppression. They named a white man president of the convention and acknowledged the value of advice of those who had experience in governing. As one delegate put it: "We must unite our white fellow citizens. Can we afford to lose from the councils of state our first men? No, fellow citizens, no! We want only the best and ablest men. And then with a strong pull, and a long pull, and a pull together, up goes South Carolina." In this spirit, the delegates undertook to reconstruct their state.

The Constitution of 1868

The new constitution which they ratified was completed in March, 1868, and it was regarded as so sound a document that it was not changed for twenty years after Radical Reconstruction came to an end. The Black Code was abolished, South Carolinians (black and white) no longer had to own property in order to vote, men could no longer be sent to jail for nonpayment of debts, provision for divorce and other enlargements of the rights of women were achieved. It was the most democratic constitution South Carolina had ever had. One of its finest provisions was for the system of free public schools advocated by Robert Smalls.

Free and Integrated Public Schools

The short, strong pilot, his face bearded in the best style of the day and wearing a bow tie, which his wife knew was fitting for a man in important public service, stood up and offered a resolution to the convention early in its meeting. He read his speech; it was formal and it was eloquent:

> Whereas, the maintenance of an intelligent government, faithful to the interest and liberties of the people, must in great measure depend upon the intelligence of the people themselves and, Whereas, the experience of those states which have opened to the poor and rich alike the opportunities of instruction has demonstrated the utility of common schools in elevating the intellectual character of their population, therefore, Resolved, that the Committee on the Constitution be directed to report an article providing for a system of common schools, of different grades, to be open without charge to all classes of persons.

Smalls' resolution was passed. South Carolina, which had not provided education for its white children who were poor and had made it a crime to educate Negro children at all, was to have a public school system. During Radical Reconstruction, Negroes attended the University of South Carolina, which had long been one of the South's best schools.

The constitution was ratified and Robert Smalls spent the next seven years, first as his district's representative and then as its state senator, in the legislature at Columbia, the state capital. He served on several committees, including those concerned with taxation and the operation of the state penitentiary. He gave strong support to the schools he had done so much to establish, advocating large appropriations for them. Smalls, a general in the state militia, vice chairman of the Republican party in South Carolina, and a delegate to his party's national convention when Ulysses S. Grant was nominated for President, was a member of the legislature in Columbia when James Shepherd Pike paid a visit in 1873.

The End of Radical Reconstruction

Robert Smalls was one of the twenty-two Negroes elected to Congress in the post-Civil War period. He took his seat in 1875, but in the election of 1886, using methods which will be examined in the next chapter, the white Democrats prevented the Negroes from voting and claimed that a member of one of the old white planter families of the Sea Islands, William Elliott, was elected to Congress in Smalls' place. The election was contested and the House of Representatives debated the issue and then voted — to give Smalls' seat to Elliott. In the debate, a young Wisconsin Congressman, Robert LaFollette, sternly told his colleagues: "You say in justification that the Negro is ignorant, inferior, incapable of growth. Secretly, do you not fear the opposite? Is it against the dull and submissive that you direct your hardest blows? Or are they aimed at these who, like Robert Smalls, have shown intellect, courage and determination to lift their people to a higher level and maintain their rights as free men?"[12]

QUESTIONS

1. How well did the Constitutional Convention and the integrated legislature represent the interests of the Negroes of South Carolina? How did it represent the interests of all South Carolinians?

2. Does the corruption of the South Carolina legislature justify the subsequent barring of the Negro from effective politics?

---

[12]*Ibid.*, p. 224.

SUGGESTED READING

The great Negro historian, W. E. B. DuBois, refocused attention on the positive aspects of Reconstruction with *Black Reconstruction* (New York, 1935) but he did not convince many white historians to abandon James Pike, whose work was reissued in that same year with the famous illustrations by Thomas Nast from *Harpers,* Henry Steele Commager, ed., James S. Pike, *The Prostrate Years* (New York, 1935). John Hope Franklin, another important Negro historian, invited a new look at the subject in *Reconstruction After the Civil War* (Chicago, 1961), and Joel Williamson's *After Slavery: The Negro in South Carolina During Reconstruction, 1861-1877* (Chapel Hill, 1965) is an excellent example of the work, sympathetic to the Negro, which is now being done.

chapter 5

A Revolution Compromised

Introduction

If the Negroes of the South took as active a part in politics during Reconstruction, as we have seen they did, why has it been necessary to have civil rights marches in our time to encourage the Negroes in the South to register to vote? Why has it been necessary to send federal registrars into Southern states to see to it that the black voters register? Why, when there were once Negro senators and congressmen, lieutenant governors, and speakers of state houses of representatives, does it become national news when a Negro is elected to a seat in his state's legislature?

The way the conservative white Southerners regained domination over their region from the Negroes and radical white men who were willing to engage in politics with them was to stage a counterrevolution. The battle involved politics, to be sure, but it also involved the use of violence. Many Negroes were killed.

Radical Reconstruction — Black Reconstruction — had brought about revolutionary social change. Less than a decade after they were slaves, Negroes were participating in the governing of their region. Their old masters were among the governed. When the counterrevolution was completed in 1877, the radicals and the Negroes had been routed. Negroes were not driven from politics completely — that came thirty years later — but from 1877 on the white men ruled supreme.

The "Mississippi Plan"

The return of the white Southerners to supremacy was accomplished somewhat differently in each of the states. As we have noted in our chapter on the "black" legislatures, there was no Southern state which ever had a black governor, and only one which had a Negro majority in its legislature. Virginia never had Radical Reconstruction in the way her sister states knew it. But the reassertion elsewhere of white domination followed similar patterns, and the way it was accomplished in Mississippi during the election of 1875 earned the name the "Mississippi Plan." It was a plan which was followed in the last three states to have radical governments. In the election of 1876, South Carolinians, led by aristocratic Wade Hampton and his Red Shirts, unseated all the Negro Congressmen except Robert Smalls, who was saved for another ten years only by his personal popularity in an overwhelmingly black district. Florida and Louisiana were similarly "redeemed," and the last three states were restored to the old Southern leadership. Let us have a look, then, at Mississippi and the counterrevolution of 1875.

In the case of the Memphis riot in 1866, the response of the federal government had been to grant political power to the Negro so that he could protect himself in his own state. This political power, however, did not stop the violence which was often instigated by the Ku Klux Klan, a secret society dedicated to reestablishing the domination of white men over the Negroes. This organization had been founded in 1866 and its hooded members, riding at night, attacked Negroes whom they deemed insolent, killing or mutilating them. The Klan's record for ferocity established, other Negroes were left in terror and often intimidated to the point of not asserting their rights. Three times during the Grant administration, Congress passed bills (one of which was used in the case of the murdered Civil Rights workers in Philadelphia, Mississippi, in 1964) aimed at using federal power to quell such terrorist activities. As late as 1876, President Grant called out troops whose presence ended a terrorist campaign in South Carolina in which several Negroes had been killed.

The threat of federal intervention had dissuaded conservative white Mississippians from threatening the Negroes with violence as a means of regaining control of their state. The first governor under Radical Reconstruction had a paternal attitude toward the Negroes, but did regard governing as a white man's job. When, in the election of 1873, a New Englander and a truly radical carpetbagger, Adelbert Ames, was elected governor and many Negroes became officeholders, the white supremacists stopped being cautious.

White Men Faced with Ostracism

The redeemers, as the white supremacists were known, organized quietly but efficiently. Their first targets were the white men who were members of the Republican party and willing to cooperate with the Negroes in politics. The weapon here was social ostracism. A man who had long been a leader in his community and had accepted the fact of the Civil War and the changed status of the Negroes suddenly found that his white neighbors would not even nod to him in the street. The closing of social doors meant the closing of economic ones as well. The technique worked in many cases. As one Mississippian put it, his children's future depended on his deserting a cause he knew to be right — and so the sacrifice was made.

An Election Purpose Stated

Social ostracism was not enough. The redeemer newspapers in Mississippi began a major attack on Negro suffrage and its alleged disastrous effects. That black Mississippians were firmly established as voters was admitted.

The strategy was to push them out of the way. "The way to treat Sambo is not to argue with him or to reason with him. If you do that, it puffs his vanity and it only makes him insolent. Say to him, 'Here, we are going to *carry* this election; you may vote as you like; but we *are* going to carry it,' " said one newspaper editor.[1]

Electioneering at the South.   *(The Bettmann Archive, Inc.)*

An Economic Threat

An ominous note had been introduced into Mississippi's 1875 campaign. The Negroes soon learned that to vote as they liked would entail a great risk. They were threatened that if they voted Republican (the Radical integrated party) they would lose their jobs. Any vote for a Republican was assumed to have been cast by a Negro; the punishment was the firing of all freedmen who had voted. Eventually, as the redeemers calculated it, the need for a job would force Negroes to persuade all their brothers to withdraw from political activity in support of integrationist candidates. Even the repeal of the Black Code had not resulted in the mass of Mississippi Negroes gaining their own farms and, as most of them worked for white planters, this economic threat was a serious one. The dependence of the Negroes on white men in the community then was underscored when doctors threatened not to care for black patients who voted Republican.

---

[1]Quoted in Vernon Lane Wharton, *The Negro in Mississippi: 1865-1890* (New York, 1947), p. 184.

In counties with a large black population majority, the Democrats could not be confident that scaring the Negroes into staying away from the polls would do the job. In these counties, strenuous efforts were made to convince the Negroes to vote for the Democrats. One device for achieving this was for the white supremacists to issue badges to Negroes pledged to vote for the Democrats. If worn, these badges would ensure the wearer's safety.

An Election Machine Effectively Organized

As the election drew nearer, even these nonviolent forms of coercion were deemed insufficient. The supremacist newspapers now took up the slogan: "Carry the election peaceably if we can, forcibly if we must."[2] Governor Ames was much worried about the prospect of bloodshed. He felt that he could not send in the state militia to keep order as the only citizens he could get to join the militia were Negroes and he feared a racial war. His aim was to convince the private white groups who owned arms not to use them, promising in return to keep the Negro militia undeployed. The failure of this effort by the governor is suggested by a newspaper account of what happened in Monroe County: "As the central power [the governor] made treaties in Jackson [the state capital] involving the laying down or stacking arms, the people in this part of the state burnished their arms and bought more cartridges, . . . each county conducted the campaign upon its own plan . . . each looking to winning its own home fight in its own way, and each ready and willing to support its neighbors physically and morally. . . .

". . . here and elsewhere in the dark counties, we guaranteed peace by thoroughly organizing for war; and . . . at the call of the County Executive Committee it was very easy — as demonstrated on several occasions — to put seventeen hundred well-mounted horsemen into line. . . . In addition to this, our eight hundred square miles of territory was so thoroughly connected by courier lines and posts, that we could communicate with every voter within its borders within a few hours."[3] The redeemer organization was state-wide and effective.

Negroes who persisted in their efforts to campaign in the election were reminded of the Meridan "riot" of 1871 in which, as one white participant put it, "every man that could do so got a gun or a pistol and went on the hunt for negroes. . . . " It was not known how many Negroes were killed by the enraged whites, but the number has been estimated at from twenty-five to thirty. However, despite the example of Meridan, many black people refused to withdraw from politics in 1875.

Help from Washington

As the election drew near, Governor Ames, more troubled than ever at the prospect of bloodshed on election day, got in touch with the Attorney General of the United States, Edwards Pierrepont, and asked for federal

---

[2]*Ibid.*, p. 187.
[3]*Ibid.*, pp. 187-188.

help. Ames wrote: "Let the odium, in all its magnitude descend on me. I cannot escape. I am conscious in the discharge of my duty toward a class of American citizens whose only offense consists in their color, and which I am powerless to protect."

As Vernon Lane Wharton, from whom this account of the Mississippi election of 1875 is drawn, tells it, Ames' request was doomed. "The plea was hopeless. Negro suffrage, or even Negro freedom, had never been popular with the masses in the North. Negro suffrage had appeared to be necessary, and had been accepted as such. . . . Its maintenance had proved to be a troublesome problem. Why should the Negro majority in Mississippi be constantly crying for help? The sending of federal troops into a state simply to prevent white men from ruling Negroes was distasteful to the average Northern voter. In the final moment of his decision, Grant was visited by a delegation of politicians from Ohio, a pivotal state which was to have an election in October. Mississippi, these visitors declared, was already lost to the party; troops would arrive too late to save the state. Even worse, the order that sent troops to Mississippi would mean the loss of Ohio to the [Republican] party. The Negroes must be sacrificed. Grant's answer to Ames was a statement that aid could not be sent until all local resources had been exhausted. In the midst of the negotiations, [Attorney General] Pierrepont declared, "The whole public was tired of these annual autumnal outbreaks in the South."[4]

Election Day

On election day, the Negroes in many parties of Mississippi were alarmed. One black Republican had written to Governor Ames from Yazoo City: "I beg you most fulley [sic] to send the United soldiers here; they have hung six more men since the killing of Mr. Fawn; they won't let the republican have no ticket. . . ." Ames had no federal troops to send. The Democrats swept the election. In Yazoo County, with a heavy Negro population majority, the Republicans got seven votes. In Kemper County, they received four votes; in Tishomingo, twelve. Only Negro Congressman John R. Lynch, held his seat. The Democrats made great gains in county offices and won control of the state legislature. In the only state-wide contest, the Democratic candidate for state treasurer beat a popular Confederate general running on the Republican ticket. Mississippi was redeemed.

The National Election of 1876

During the presidential election of 1876, America's centennial and the anniversary also of its promise of equality, three Southern states remained unredeemed. These states, South Carolina, Florida, and Louisiana, all elected redemptionist governors in 1876. In all three states, versions of the Mississippi Plan were used to accomplish the victory.

No such clear-cut victory was available to a Presidential candidate. Neither Republican Rutherford B. Hayes from Ohio nor Democrat Samuel

---

[4]*Ibid.*, pp. 193-194.

Tilden from New York had a majority in the Electoral College because of disputed returns in three Southern states. Conservative Democrats, now victorious in state elections in Louisiana, South Carolina, and Florida, claimed that their votes for Tilden should be counted. Radical Republicans in these states, making their last bid for power, argued that their slate of electors should be counted.

Many people in the nation were afraid that the stress of the tied election might bring the nation to disunion. A commission of distinguished citizens was chosen to decide which votes should be counted and resolve the national dilemma. Fraud on both sides was easily discerned, and so the decision on which slates were to be counted was made in secret negotiations between conservative Southern Democrats and Republicans close to Hayes.

The resolution of the problem is called the Compromise of 1877. It was another of the great nineteenth-century sectional compromises, similar in result to the Missouri Compromise of 1820 and the Compromise of 1850. Again the Union was secured and the Negro sacrificed. In 1877, the Democrats agreed to drop the claim of their electors in the three disputed states and allow Tilden to be defeated and Hayes elected. In return, the Republicans agreed to support legislation in Congress favorable to Southern railroads. In a move more symbolic than real, they also agreed to remove the federal troops from the South. (As we have seen in Mississippi, none were available where they were needed.) Finally, and of lasting importance to the Negroes of the South and the nation, the Republicans acquiesced to the redemption of the last three Southern states. Hereafter, decisions concerning the nations' Negroes were left to the conservative white governments of the Southern states.

QUESTIONS

1. Were white Southerners justified in their attempt to remove their former slaves from an active role in politics?

2. If you had been President Grant when the request for help came from Governor Ames, what would you have done?

3. Do you think Negroes would be better off today if Grant had sent the troops Ames had requested?

SUGGESTED READING

The definitive study of the national compromise which ended Radical Reconstruction and the hopes of the Negroes to participate in the determination of their own political future is C. Vann Woodward's *Reunion and Reaction: The Compromise of 1877 and the End of Reconstruction* (New York, 1956.) The account in this chapter of the redemption of one Southern state by white supremacists is from Vernon Lane Wharton's *The Negro in Mississippi, 1865-1890* (New York, 1965).

chapter 6

The Freedmen As Farmers

Introduction

"Aside from the question of race and status, perhaps the greatest weakness of the negro population in 1865 was its extreme poverty."[1] This was the judgment of Walter L. Fleming, an early historian of Reconstruction, and it is not unlike that of a present-day economist who has said that the maintenance of full employment is "the single most important step" the nation can take to help the Negro.[2] Both observers regard the Negro's economic need as a crucial one. This chapter examines the economic problems the freedmen faced.

The Lands of the South

The first Negroes were brought to America as a cheap source of agricultural labor. When slavery was stopped two and a half centuries later, most Negroes in the country were still farm workers. There were some attempts made to find ways for the ex-slaves to earn a living in industry, but for the most part Americans, black and white, expected that the lands of the South, on which most Negroes in the country had always lived, would provide the key to their future. And so, until the emigration to the cities in the 20th century, the lands of the South were where the Negroes stayed.

The great question was how well these lands on which Negro Americans had always lived as slaves would provide for them as freedmen. It has already been noted that they were not awarded forty acres and a mule by the government so that they could start out as independent farmers. Those freedmen with just the forty acres (and even the mule) but without a plow and hoes and without cash to buy seed and fertilizer very likely would have lost their farms to creditors or land speculators. As will be seen below

---

[1] Walter L. Fleming, *The Freedman's Savings Bank: A Chapter in the Economic History of the Negro Race* (Chapel Hill, 1927), p. 2.
[2] James Tobin, quoted in I. F. Stone, "The Negro American," *New York Review of Books,* August 10, 1966, p. 8.

in the discussion of the lien merchants, there was little chance for the freed-men to escape from economic bondage. But there *was* a chance. On the Sea Islands, a small band of Northerners had tried to help the freedmen start out as independent farmers. The man in charge of these experiments, Rufus Saxton, angrily — but in vain — cried out that the freedmen had earned such farms by "the sweat of their brow through generations of labor" as slaves. Was he right in feeling that the nation should have made it federal policy to set the freedmen up on working farms of their own?

Sharecropping

The government did not shoulder its responsibility as Saxton wanted it to and the grant of farms was not made. This chapter traces the efforts of the freedmen to work out for themselves a kind of independence on the land within a system called *sharecropping*. By the time Reconstruction was over, most Negroes in the South were sharecroppers; in 1900, 75.3 percent of all Negro farmers in the South were either "croppers" or tenants.[3]

A Farm of Your Own. As one of Saxton's fellow officers of the Freed-men's Bureau had told the members of the Joint Committee on Reconstruc-tion in 1866, the Negroes had "almost a passion" for land. This was not the product of a sentimental attraction to the land itself. They wanted the security which any nineteenth-century man thought came from the ownership of one's own house and farm. As the previous chapters showed, there were attempts by military commanders during the war and by the Congress in the earliest days of Reconstruction to put farms in the hands of the freedmen. This was frustrated by President Johnson, who even sent the head of the freedmen's own agency to tell the Negro farmers of Edisto that they must give up their farms. The Negroes of the Sea Islands strongly resisted this plea that they accept the loss of their farms. To comply was to agree to go back to work for the same man who had been their master during slavery.

Although their new work contracts were to be policed by the Freedmen's Bureau, this was not enough to reassure the Negroes of neighboring Wad-malaw Island. Leaving crops standing in the fields, the Negro farm families crowded into boats and rowed themselves over to Savannah. They were willing to risk the threat of unemployment in an unfamiliar town rather than return to work under the discipline of the old master.

A Replacement for Slavery

Most Negro families in the South did not rebel in this way. Unlike the Sea Islanders, who were given a rare opportunity when their owners fled, other ex-slaves never had the taste of farming on their own without any contact with their old masters. When it became clear after the war that the government was not going to break up the huge plantations into forty-acre homesteads, the Negro farmers, like the white planters, had to face the problem of raising a crop to keep themselves fed and clothed.

---

[3]C. Vann Woodward, *Origins of the New South 1877-1913* (Baton Rouge, 1951), p. 206.

On June 1, 1865, two months after the Civil War ended and in the middle of the crop-raising season, two Mississippians came before an officer of the Union army. One was a planter named L. F. Thomson who wanted to be sure the cotton in the field would be harvested. Accompanying Thomson was Luther R. Mills, a Negro "which he lately owned." Mills, now no longer a slave, had to provide for his wife, Martha, and three young children. Thomson and Mills had come to execute a contract.[4]

On a piece of paper torn from an envelope, the Union officer wrote in pencil a document stating that Mills and his wife had been told "of their freedom and that they could hire themselves to who they chose but that said freedmen agreed to remain and work for said Thomson during the present year and for their rations and clothing in the usual way before the war." The fears of the family being separated by sale, as had been possible during slavery, were past for the Mills, but otherwise they would go on living just as they had as slaves.

As Luther Mills could not write, the planter Thomson assisted his former slave by signing for him too. "Luther" is written on the document in the same hand just below "L. F. Thomson."

Federally Approved Contracts

As has been noted, the federal government failed to supply the Mills family and other Negroes with forty acres at the end of 1865 and so, at the beginning of the new year, Mills again was faced with the necessity of continuing to care for his family on someone else's land. On January 1, 1866, now using a printed form provided by the Freedmen's Bureau, Thomson signed a new contract, and so did Mills, this time signing with an "X." Thomson agreed to provide the Mills family with, "free of charge, clothing and food of good quality and sufficient quantity; good and sufficient quarters and medical attendance when necessary, and kind and humane treatment, to allot to them . . . for garden purposes," [and here the blank space in the form was filled in with the words] "a patch."

The "patch"

The patch, a bit of ground on which the Negro farmer could grow vegetables for his family, was a carryover from slavery. It was also the cornerstone on which the sharecropping system was built. It soon appeared to the Mills that the only way to make their lives tolerable was to extend the patch and make it big enough to raise a crop large enough to supply them with the few other goods they needed, besides the vegetables and the food provided by the hogs and chickens they raised, to keep alive.

"A Third of Crop Raised." The patch had not yet grown to these proportions in the contract which Thomson and Mills signed in January, 1867. Under that arrangement, the planter, as under slavery, assumed responsibility for the care of the Mills and other Negro families still living

---

[4]From contracts on file in Records of Bureau of Refugees, Freedman and Abandoned Lands, National Archives.

in their slave cabins. But unlike the penciled contract of the previous spring, Thomson now agreed that at the end of the crop year, Mills was to have "a third of crop raised" in return for his labor. The other two-thirds was the planter's. In some other contracts — those most favored by Yankee businessmen who were satisfied by the economic system in the industrial North — the planter agreed to pay his workers cash wages. In many cases, these wages were paid only at the end of the crop season.

During the long months of hard labor before the cotton was baled, the Negro workers knew that any reward for their labor depended on their satisfying the planter. All of the paternalism of slavery remained in force. The system provided security — a house, care, clothes, food — and it called for discipline. There is evidence that Thomson had been a kind "old massa" and white society expected a gentleman to be such, but there was nothing to ensure that he was. And there was not much to ensure that he would be a kind "new massa" in the post-war South.

The Freedmen's Bureau thought that it could convince the planters to be kind. Indeed, the presence of Bureau agents all over the South made it look as if the federal government was going to insist on it, but the Negroes soon found that not only did they have to endure the old paternalism they knew all too well but they had to get used to a Yankee stepfather as well.

The Freedmen's Bureau

The Freedmen's Bureau agent, a young Union army officer lonely in a farm town deep in the South, had found to his surprise that not all former rebels in the country treated him with contempt. The white farmers, he

A Freedmen's Bureau agent (right) hears both planters and freedmen.

(The Bettmann Archive, Inc.)

discovered, were much like the people he had known back home. They looked like people he knew; they got the same pleasure out of saddling up a horse and riding far into the country; they even discovered that their cousins in Cincinnati knew each other. When the Southern farmer — Thomson, or most any other — told the Union soldier about his troubles keeping the Negroes hard at work, the Yankee, who found his black Freedmen's Bureau clients hard to understand, was sympathetic. If Luther Mills were to come into the Bureau office to complain of a beating which had been inflicted on him by Thomson, it was very likely that the agent already knew another version of the incident. Men like Thomson, who had known Negroes all their lives, undertook to explain them. Thomson may well have told the agent that despite the fact that his contract said that "tools were to be kept in good repair," Mills had broken four hoe handles. The agent would learn that this was a form of insubordination frequently resorted to under slavery. The Bureau agent, aware of cases of starvation in areas where there had been crop failures, agreed with Thomson that work stoppages could not be allowed.

In answer to a complaint about the severity of his treatment by the planter, Mills was apt to receive a sermon from the agent on the virtue of hard work and the importance of cooperating with his former master. Only by being diligent in his labor, the freedman was told, could he prove himself worthy to be free.

A Measure of Freedom

Luther Mills and others soon learned that only by insisting on the relative freedom available to them as croppers or tenants could they avoid the discipline of a field gang. The arrangements varied over the South, but gradually the Negro farmers convinced their former masters to enlarge the "patch" so that the freedman and his family could raise his own crop of cotton. If the arrangement called simply for the use of the land by the Negro in return for delivering to the planter the larger portion of the cotton raised, it was known as sharecropping. Sometimes the arrangement was more formal and a legal tenancy was established, which called for the payment of rent either in bales of cotton or cash raised from the sale of cotton.

The planters acquiesced to the shares system not because it was perfect, but because it appeared a workable system for maintaining their ownership of the land of the South. It relieved the planters of the paternal responsibilities of slavery and the contract system. It also meant that fewer hoes would be broken (although most of the time the hoes, the plows, and the mules continued to be owned by the owner of the land). The Negro farmers were free from the disciplines of a planter serving as overseer. Now Mills was on his own, but if he was to get the third or half of the crop to sell to keep his family going, he had to work hard. He had to learn to discipline himself.

The master, by owning the land, the mule, and the plow, strictly limited this freedom, but there was a point beyond which he could no longer invade the Mills' lives. The sharecropper had to get himself up in the morning, he had to plant his seed, hoe his field, and pick his cotton himself. If he was lazy and the crop was small, the owner's share of the cotton would be small and so would his. Poverty was his punishment, but whippings as part of a field gang no longer were.

The Lien System

As if the stringent economies of the sharecropper system were not enough of a burden to both the cropper and the owner of the land, there grew up in the South a vicious system of farm financing. Called the *lien system,* it spread, says C. Vann Woodward, "like Jimson weed, a curse to the soil."[5] Farmers in the South had to have credit to buy seeds and tools, and the lien system was the only way in which credit was available in the South, which had little capital and was a dependent colonial economy supplying raw material to the industrial North. "The system," writes Woodward, "did hold together with financial bailing wire the shattered machinery of Southern agriculture — liberated slave, bankrupt planter, and supply merchant — in sufficient co-ordination to support life, but it represented one of the strangest contractual relationships in the history of finance."[6] It is Woodward's contention that the lien system, which held all its participants in continual bondage, "divorced landownership from its age-old prerogatives."

As for the Negro tenant farmer, he "seemed to prefer the more remote . . . control of the lien-merchant peonage to the immediate control of the planter."[7] It is probable that even if more of the freedmen had been granted forty acres and a mule by the government right at the end of the Civil War — had become landowners — they would still have slipped into the same bondage that the sharecroppers and tenants knew in their relations with the merchants. The farmers would have needed not only the mule but hoes, seed, fertilizer and, with no accumulated capital, the freedmen could only have gotten these at the merchant's store.

No Way Out

If a farmer, disgusted with his unpromising life, decided one year to work especially hard and make enough money to move his family away, he more than likely found that he had borrowed so much money (perhaps less than $100, but a lot to him) to get the few tools he needed that at the end of the season his bill with the merchant was larger than his profit. At this point, the farmer's only way to meet his debt was to give up his dream of moving and agree to stay and raise another crop, on which the merchant held a lien, to pay the money he owed. And then when the next crop season came, the farmer would have to borrow still more from the merchant to get seed for the new crop and the entrapping circle closed around him again.

---

[5]Woodward, *Origins of the New South,* p. 180.
[6]*Ibid.,* p. 180.
[7]*Ibid.,* p. 184.

A Century after Emancipation

Today the descendents of Luther Mills still live on the same land in Mississippi. The house is a different one, but it is hardly changed in appearance. Chickens scratch in the dry dirt around its uncertain foundation stones. An ancient washing machine on the porch may be the only symbol of advance into the twentieth century. The shrunken slats of the unpainted building are outlined with dark cracks. Inside, the walls are papered with newspapers and pages from magazines, there are two scraps of incompatibly patterned linoleum on the floor, and the simple chairs and table and beds are battered. There is a sag to the building which tells you it will not last forever; there is a hesitation to its slant which reminds you that houses usually last longer than the people who live in them.

(Ewing Galloway)

The Mills are still sharecroppers although the Thomsons have long since ceased to be their landlords. The Mills are dependent on the present owner of the land on which their house stands. The land is still not theirs and they share the crop with the owner. The Mills are dependent too on the white man's store where they buy their seed and staples on credit, paying the storekeeper when the crop is sold. If the Mills should cross the owner of their land or the storekeeper, if, for example, they should participate in the Civil Rights movement discussed later, they risk losing their house, their way of earning a living, and supplies to keep their family fed and clothed. In a nation encrusted with the benefits of being rich, the income of these people (and there are many white Southerners in the same economic position) is measurable in hundreds rather than thousands or tens of thousands of dollars.

Now mechanical farming equipment available in the deep South is making the always marginal farm operations of the sharecroppers obsolete. Already many thousands of croppers have had to give up and move to Northern cities. Soon sharecropping may be over, but it will be accomplished by dispersal of the Negroes. The lands they worked for so many generations never yielded the strength to overcome what has been called their greatest liability on entering freedom at the end of the Civil War — their "extreme poverty." Had these lands been used to provide the freedmen with working farms — not only forty acres but also the mule and equipment and money to buy starting supplies with — poverty might not have been so overwhelmingly the continuing condition of America's Negroes. In an important sense, for a man to have a working farm of his own in nineteenth-century America was for him to have equality. This the sharecroppers — then and now — do not enjoy.

QUESTIONS

1. Were the sharecropper and the crop lien farmer significantly freer than the slave?

2. Do you think that the majority of Negroes would be significantly better off today if they had been given farms in 1865?

3. Should the United States government have given each family of freedmen forty acres, a mule, and all that was needed to make a farm workable as back wages for slavery?

SUGGESTED READING

There is no adequate study of the beginning of the sharecropping system or on agriculture in the South, in general, during Reconstruction. C. Vann Woodward's *Origins of the New South, 1877-1913* (Baton Rouge, 1951) is the best study of the region during this period. It handsomely describes how poorly the Negroes — and most white farmers — fared in the South. A famous account of sharecropping is James Agee's and Walker Evans' *Let Us Praise Famous Men* (Baton Rouge, 1941). Another perceptive book is Herman Clarence Nixon's *Forty Acres and Steel Mules* (Chapel Hill, 1938).

chapter 7

"Separate But Equal"

Introduction

It will be recalled that the 14th Amendment, drawn up the year after the Civil War, had seemed to some to offer the Negro a promise of true equality. In 1875, Justice Samuel Miller, speaking for the Supreme Court, said that the amendment existed specifically to assist the freedmen in their post-slavery problems — for "that race and that emergency."[1] Very soon, however, the Negroes of the South were to learn just how slight was the help that they could expect from the 14th Amendment.

In keeping with Justice Miller's statement of purpose, the Congress had, in 1870, passed a series of four force bills which were designed to protect the Negroes' rights. One of these bills, directed specifically at the Ku Klux Klan, stated that it was an offense punishable by fine or imprisonment for "two or more persons . . . [to] band or conspire together, or go in disguise upon the public highway . . . with intent to . . . intimidate any citizen, with intent to prevent or hinder his free exercise and enjoyment of any right or privilege guarded or secured to him by the Constitution or laws of the United States. . . ."[2]

The Cruikshank and Harris Cases

Having already heard, in Justice Miller's words, the resolve of the federal government to protect the Negroes, and having seen, in the force bills, the establishment of a potentially effective means of carrying out this resolve, let us then look at how the government did, in fact, proceed.

Negroes in Louisiana claimed that they had been subjected to threats to keep them from voting, but the Supreme Court could find no grounds for punishing the Klansmen for making such threats. In its decision in *U.S.*

---

[1] *Slaughter-House Cases* (1873) 16 Wallace 36, p. 81.
[2] *United States Statutes at Large,* Vol. 16, 1869-71, May 31, 1870, "An Act to enforce the Right of Citizens of the United States to vote in the several States of this Union, and for other Purposes," p. 141.

v. Cruikshank, the Court said that the allegations were "too vague," and that it was the state of Louisiana which must guarantee its citizens rights; the federal government (Congress notwithstanding) had no right to do so.[3] Louisiana was reminded that: "Every republican government is in duty bound to protect all its citizens. . . . That duty was originally assumed by the States; and it still remains there. The only obligation resting upon the United States," said the Court, "is to see that the States do not deny the right."[4] But the Supreme Court did not suggest any way which would force Louisiana or any other state to do its duty to its citizens.

In 1883, the Court again considered the fact that Negroes often were not safe in their own communities. In Crockett County, Tennessee, P. M. Wells and three other Negroes were arrested for an alleged criminal offense, jailed, and held for trial. The white "yeomen" (as the court reporter called them) of Crockett County, so enraged by the crime of which the Negroes were accused, banded together to take the law into their own hands. Led by deputy sheriff R. W. Harris, at least twenty men broke into the jail where the blacks were awaiting trial. They took the Negro prisoners from their cell and carried them out into the country. There, the Negroes were beaten so severely that one of them, Wells, died.

When the case reached the Supreme Court, the justices ruled that the 14th Amendment provided for the protection of people only if they were harmed by direct action of the state. The Court ruled that Harris and his band were merely private citizens. Neither the acquiescence of a public official (or sheriff) to the violence nor Tennessee's failure to protect its prisoners was held to be a state action contrary to the spirit of the 14th Amendment. For now, far from being a shield for the Negro, the Court saw the amendment as "not a guarantee against the commission of individual offenses"; moreover, the Court declared, "the power of Congress does not extend to the passage of laws for suppression of crime within the states."[5]

The Civil Rights Cases

Also in 1883, the Court made it clear that not only equal protection but other privileges available to white citizens of the nation were not equally available to Negroes. On November 22, 1879, William R. Davis, a Negro, bought two reserved tickets to the Grand Opera House in New York City for a production of Victor Hugo's *Ruy Blas,* starring Edwin Booth. When Davis got to the theater, he was told his tickets were no good and that his money would be refunded. Davis protested, citing the Civil Rights Bill of 1875, which specifically said that Negroes could not be denied admission to a place of public accommodation on account of their color. His case reached the Supreme Court with similar ones involving the denial of a meal to a Negro in a hotel in Topeka, Kansas, the denial of the admission of

[3]*United States v. Cruikshank* (1876) 92 US 542, pp. 543-544.
[4]*Ibid.,* p. 555.
[5]*United States v. Harris* (1883) 106 US 629, p. 638.

a Negro to the dress circle of a theater in San Francisco, and the barring of Negroes from first-class cars on railroads in Tennessee and Virginia.[6]

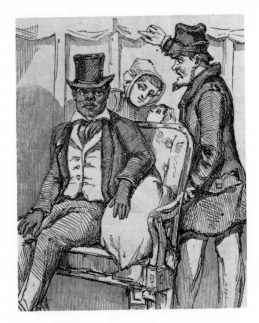

Negro expulsion from railway car: Philadelphia.

(The Bettmann Archive, Inc.)

Justice Joseph Bradley of New Jersey, speaking for a court on which Justice Miller still sat, followed the reasoning of the Cruikshank and Harris cases and declared the Civil Rights Acts unconstitutional. Only the acts of states preventing equal protection of the laws to Negroes were prohibited by the 14th Amendment. Private citizens who owned theaters or hotels were at liberty to deny access to their facilities to Negroes if they so desired.[7]

The only dissenting voice came from the only Southerner and the one man on the court who had once owned slaves, Justice John Marshall Harlan. Said Harlan: "Today, it is the colored race which is denied, by corporation and individuals wielding public authority, rights fundamental in their freeddom and citizenship. At some future time, it may be that some other race will fall under the ban of race discrimination. If the constitutional amendments be enforced, according to the intent with which, as I conceive, they were adopted, there cannot be, in this republic, any class of human beings in practical subjugation to another class."[8]

---

[6]Alan F. Weston, "The Case of the Prejudiced Doorkeeper," John A. Garraty, ed., *Quarrels That Have Shaped the Constitution,* (New York, 1962), pp. 128-144.

[7]*Civil Rights Cases* (1883) 109 US 3, pp. 8-26.

[8]*Ibid.,* p. 62.

Jim Crow

As we have seen in the decision in the *Civil Rights Cases,* the Supreme Court extended its flight from protection of the Negro to the point where it found itself powerless to prevent private acts of discrimination. It is to this tendency of racial separation, of segregation, that we give the name of Jim Crow. We must be aware, however, that Jim Crow had his origins in the North. For while the South certainly had its own system of caste differentiation between whites and Negroes, the slave system made close interracial contact an everyday affair. Only with the abolition of slavery did the white Southerners discover the need for an artificial distinction between themselves and the Negroes; at this point only did the Southern whites begin their Jim Crow policy of actively differentiating between those places where Negroes and whites were permitted to go.

It had surprised a cosmopolitan Northerner, Charles Dudley Warner, to see Negroes and whites mingling freely at the exhibits of the World's Fair in New Orleans in 1885, six years after William Davis was denied a chance to see Edwin Booth perform in New York.[9] But such equality was not to last long, for Jim Crow was soon to grow in strength until his power was felt everywhere in the South and also throughout much of the North.

Moreover, Jim Crow had developed a new source of strength: whereas before he reigned merely by the whim of private theater and hotel owners, now his strength came to be derived from the acts of state legislatures.

It was on the railroads, however, that Jim Crow rode to his greatest triumph. Florida passed the first effective law separating Negroes from whites on its trains in 1887. By 1892, nine Southern states had followed suit. Virginia and the two Carolinas did not do so until the twentieth century. The sophisticated and talented Negroes of New Orleans, who had fought so hard during Reconstruction to gain equality, battled to prevent this new encroachment on their rights and brought a test case to the Supreme Court to determine the constitutionality of the state laws. The Negro who protested in the litigation — Alphonse Plessy — was very light skinned, and protested on the grounds that his most sacred right — the right to be white — had been denied him by an ordinance which recognized a color bar where human eyes could detect none. It is perhaps ironic that this kind of racism should enter a case so important to America's Negroes. However, in this case the Negroes were to see destroyed their last hope for protection under the 14th Amendment: their belief that at least it prevented the states from taking direct action to abrogate their rights.

Plessy v. Ferguson

When the case of Alphonse Plessy reached the Supreme Court, the Negroes learned that they were wrong. The 1895 decision in the famous case of *Plessy v. Ferguson* was given by Justice Henry Billings Brown of Michigan. As precedent for these new laws segregating the Negroes on

[9]C. Vann Woodward, "The Case of the Louisiana Traveler," Garraty, ed., *Quarrels That Have Shaped the Constitution,* p. 145.

trains in the South, Brown cited an 1849 decision of the Massachusetts Supreme Court allowing segregation in schools in that state, and also the existence of segregation in the schools of the nation's capital allowed by the same Congress that wrote the 14th Amendment. Brown concluded that it was not a deprivation of equal protection of the laws if the Negroes were provided with "separate but equal" facilities.[10]

He concluded that Plessy's argument was fallacious because it rests on the

> . . . assumption that the enforced separation of the two races stamps the colored race with the badge of inferiority. If this is so, it is not by reason of anything found in the act, but solely because the colored race chooses to put that construction upon it. . . . The argument also assumes that social prejudices may be overcome by legislation, and that equal rights cannot be secured by the negro except by an enforced commingling of the two races. We cannot accept this proposition. . . . Legislation is powerless to eradicate racial instincts, or to abolish distinctions based upon physical differences, and the attempt to do so can only result in accentuating the difficulties of the present situation. If the civil and political rights of both races be equal, one cannot be inferior to the other civilly or politically. If one race be inferior to the other socially, the constitution of the United States cannot put them upon the same plane.[11]

Justice Harlan is Dissent

Once more, John Marshall Harlan spoke in lonely dissent. Acknowledging great pride in his own white race and suggesting that it could maintain its present level of excellence without the aid of Jim Crow, Harlan wrote:

> But in view of the constitution, in the eye of the law, there is in this country no superior, dominant, ruling class of citizens. There is no caste here. Our constitution is color-blind, and neither knows nor tolerates classes among citizens. In respect of civil rights, all citizens are equal before the law. The humblest is peer of the most powerful. The law regards man as man, and takes no account of his surroundings, or of his color when his civil rights as guaranteed by the supreme law of the land are involved. . . . We boast of the freedom enjoyed by our people above all other peoples. But it is difficult to reconcile that boast with a state of laws which, practically, puts the brand of servitude and degradation upon a large class of our fellow citizens — our equals before the law. The thin disguise of "equal" accommodations for passengers in railroad coaches will not mislead any one, nor atone for the wrong this day done.[12]

The "brutal and irritating" discriminations against American Negroes had not yet reached their peak. After the Plessy case, there were no further obstacles to state and local laws separating the races. At the close of the century in which they had gained their freedom and a taste of equality, the freedmen were to have hurled at them a barrage of statutes designed to separate them from virtually every corner of public life in which they might have expected to meet white men on a plane of equality.

The first and crucial step was to deprive the Negro of access to the polls. Through the use of one device or another (for example, a "grandfather

---

[10]*Plessy v. Ferguson* (1895) 163 US 537, pp. 540-552.
[11]*Ibid.*, p. 551.
[12]*Ibid.*, pp. 559, 562.

clause," requiring that to vote one must have had a grandfather who would have qualified as a voter), the Negroes were systematically cut off from the vote in the South. This accomplished, the elimination of the Negro's freedom to intermingle with whites in public places advanced rapidly. Laws like that which had denied Plessy his right not to be discriminated from other men now were employed to change the way of life of the entire South.

Jim Crow Triumphant

The sweep of Jim Crow's victory can be seen in the attitude of a conservative, white newspaper, the Charleston *New Courier*. The editor of this paper, thinking Jim Crow cars on railroads a silly innovation, sought to prove the absurdity of the idea by suggesting what might logically follow:

> If there must be Jim Crow cars on the railroads, there should be Jim Crow cars on the street railways. Also on all passenger boats. . . . If there are to be Jim Crow cars, moreover, there should be Jim Crow waiting saloons at all stations, and Jim Crow eating houses. . . . There should be Jim Crow sections of the jury box, and a separate Jim Crow dock and witness stand in every court — and a Jim Crow Bible for colored witnesses to kiss. It would be advisable also to have a Jim Crow section in county auditors' and treasurers' offices for the accommodation of colored taxpayers. The two races are dreadfully mixed in these offices for weeks every year, especially about Christmas. . . . There should be a Jim Crow department for making returns and paying for the privileges and blessings of citizenship. Perhaps, the best plan would be, after all, to take the short cut to the general end . . . by establishing two or three Jim Crow counties at once, and turning them over to our colored citizens for their special and exclusive accommodation.[13]

It was, however, Jim Crow who had the last laugh. Within ten years almost all the suggestions that the Charleston editor had ironically advanced — including, even, the Jim Crow Bible — had been adopted by the Southern states. In fact, many of the laws separating Negroes and whites went far beyond those imagined possible by the southern editor. C. Vann Woodward collected some examples in his book, *The Strange Career of Jim Crow:*

> In 1909 Mobile passed a curfew law applying exclusively to Negroes and requiring them to be off the streets by 10 P.M. The Oklahoma legislature in 1915 authorized its Corporation Commission to require telephone companies 'to maintain separate booths for white and colored patrons.' North Carolina and Florida required that textbooks used by the public-school children of one race be kept separate from those used by the other, and the Florida law specified separation even while the books were in storage. . . . A New Orleans ordinance segregated white and Negro prostitutes in separate districts.

> An Atlanta ordinance of . . . 1932 prohibited amateur baseball clubs of different races from playing within two blocks of each other. . . . A Birmingham ordinance got down to particulars in 1930 by making it 'unlawful for a Negro and a white person to play together or in company with each other' at dominoes or checkers.[14]

---

[13]Quoted in C. Vann Woodward, *The Strange Career of Jim Crow* (New York, 1966), pp. 49-50.
[14]Quoted in C. Vann Woodward, *The Strange Career of Jim Crow* (New York, 1966), pp. 101-102, 117-118.

Separated from white Americans by edict of the Supreme Court and by Jim Crow laws, Negro Americans were by the end of the nineteenth century searching for a new pattern of living in their land.

QUESTIONS

1. Where, if at all, in the progressive retreat from the Court's commitment to assisting the freedmen in their post-slavery problems, do you disagree with the Court's interpretation of the 14th Amendment?

2. Do Jim Crow laws seem to be a logical extension or a perversion of the separate but equal doctrine announced in *Plessy v. Ferguson?*

3. Can 'separate' ever really be 'equal'?

SUGGESTED READING

Although many Negroes today reject his views, Booker T. Washington was a most important leader of his people. His autobiography *Up from Slavery* (New York, 1901) is a key document in Negro history. John A. Garraty's *Quarrels that Have Shaped the Constitution* (New York, 1964) has readable accounts of the *Civil Rights Cases* and *Plessy v. Ferguson.* C. Vann Woodward's *The Strange Career of Jim Crow* (New York: Oxford University Press, 1966) traces the history of Jim Crow practices, showing they were not rooted in time-honored mores of the Southland, and helps dispell the myth of immutable segregation laws.

chapter 8
The Great Debate

Introduction

At the turn into the twentieth century, Negro Americans were deeply interested in one of the most famous debates in the nation's history. The discussion centered on how black Americans were to live in a land which was establishing higher and higher walls of separatism. The debate was a crucial event in the determination of the path Negroes would take in the twentieth century. Indeed, many of the issues still are argued today. The debate — it was one despite the fact that the debaters did not face each other on the same platform — was conducted by two of the most remarkable men in American history.

Booker T. Washington

Booker T. Washington was born a slave in Virginia in 1856. After emancipation, he worked in West Virginia salt furnaces and then worked his way through Hampton Institute, a school for Negroes founded in Virginia by Northern philanthropists with the help of the Freedmen's Bureau. Samuel Chapman Armstrong, the head of Hampton, had been a missionary in Hawaii and brought to his freedmen school the philosophy that he had developed in teaching the islanders. Thrift and hard work, he contended, were the ways for colored people to prove themselves in a white world.

In 1881, on Armstrong's recommendation, Washington was named principal of a school for Negro teachers in Tuskegee, Albama. He built the school from a struggling one-building operation into an educational institution that was world famous.

Even more important than Tuskegee Institute was the philosophy Washington taught there and in many speeches around the country. By the beginning of the twentieth century he was widely acclaimed by both blacks and whites as the leader of the Negro community in America. When he

Booker T. Washington.
(The Bettmann Archive, Inc.)

W. E. B. DuBois.

died in 1915 a whole nation mourned the man who had said: "No man, black or white, from North or South, shall drag me down so low as to make me hate him."

W. E. B. DuBois

W. E. B. DuBois was twelve years younger than Washington; he was born in 1868 in Great Barrington, Massachusetts. His ancestry was Negro, French Huguenot, and Dutch. He went through the public schools in his home town and then attended Fisk University, which was, like Washington's Hampton, a Negro college founded by the Freedmen's Bureau. After graduation from Fisk, he went to Harvard University where he earned his Ph.D. in 1895. He also studied in Germany and taught at Wilberforce University, the University of Pennsylvania, and from 1897-1910 at Atlanta University. His sociological studies of the Negro in Atlanta and in Philadelphia are still in use today.

It was during his years at Atlanta University that DuBois engaged in his debate with Washington. He was instrumental in the founding of the National Association for the Advancement of Colored People and edited its fighting journal, *Crisis,* from 1910 to 1932. He died in Ghana at the age of 95 in 1963.

"Cast down your bucket . . ."

At the opening of the Cotton States' Exposition in Atlanta in 1895, Booker T. Washington addressed an audience eager to see the South catch up with the North in industrial and commercial development. Washington outlined the role the Negro should play. He began with his famous parable of thirsty men at sea who were told: "Cast down your bucket where you are." Three times they refused to heed the command but finally they dropped their bucket in the salty sea and drew up fresh and sparkling water which had flowed there from the mouth of the Amazon River.[1] Washington urged black Americans to stay in America and in the South where Negroes had suffered but where "we have proved our loyalty"[2] and proudly be drawers of water.

Washington's Economic Solution

Washington called on his people to give up the struggle for equality which most white men of the South disliked. "The wisest among my race understand that the agitation of questions of social equality is the extremist folly, and that progress in the enjoyment of all the privileges that come to us must be the result of severe and constant struggle rather than of artificial forcing. No race that has anything to contribute to the markets of the world is long, in any degree, ostracized. It is important and right that all privileges of the law be ours, but it is vastly more important that we be prepared for the exercises of these privileges. The opportunity to earn a

---

[1]E. Davidson Washington, ed., *Selected Speeches of Booker T. Washington,* (New York, Doubleday, Doran and Co., 1932) p. 32.
[2]*Ibid.,* p. 34.

dollar in a factory just now is worth infinitely more than the opportunity to spend a dollar in an opera house."[3] This acceptance of inequality by black men in exchange for the promise of a measure of economic opportunity became known as the "Atlanta Compromise." It was widely acclaimed by white and black Americans as a practical answer to America's racial dilemma.

In a speech at Fisk University that same year, Washington urged Negro students to "keep a hopeful and cheerful spirit as to the future. Despite all our disadvantages and hardships, ever since our forefathers set foot upon the American soil as slaves our pathway has been marked by progress. Think of it: we went into slavery pagans; we came out Christians . . . We went into slavery without a language; we came out speaking the proud Anglo-Saxon tongue. . . .

"I believe that we are going to reach our highest development largely from the lines of scientific and industrial education."[4] Washington made his appeal to the whole of the Negro people; they were all of concern to him and he sought to reassure white Americans that they were no cause for alarm. In 1903, he said: "The Negro in this country constitutes the most compact, reliable, and peaceful element of labor, . . . if for no higher reason than the economic one, the people will see that it is worth while to keep an element of labor happy, contented, and prosperous. . . ."[5]

A Challenge to Justice

W. E. B. DuBois had a different philosophy: "The Negro race, like all races, is going to be saved by its exceptional men. The problem of education, then, among Negroes must first deal with the Talented Tenth; it is one problem of developing the Best in this race that may guide the Mass away from the contamination and death of the Worst, in their own and other races."[6] He also had a different idea about education than Washington, who stressed manual training at Tuskegee. Said DuBois: "If we make money the object of man-training, we shall develop money-makers but not necessarily men."[7] DuBois enumerated his points of difference with Washington:

"1. He is striving nobly to make Negro artisans businessmen and property owners; but it is utterly impossible, under modern competitive methods, for workingmen and property-owners to defend rights and exist without the right of suffrage.

2. He insists on thrift and self-respect, but at the same time counsels a silent submission to civic inferiority such as is bound to sap the manhood of any race in the long run."[8]

---

[3]*Ibid.*, pp. 35-36.
[4]*Ibid.*, p. 37.
[5]*Ibid.*, p. 97.
[6]Washington, DuBois and others, *The Negro Problem: A Series of Articles by Representative American Negroes of To-Day.* (New York, James Pott & Co., 1903), p. 33.
[7]*Ibid.* pp.
[8]W. E. Burghardt DuBois, *The Souls of Black Folk,* (Chicago) (A. C. McClung & Co., 1903), p. 52.

DuBois wanted not only grammar schools and manual training schools for Negroes but the upgrading of the intellectual level of Negro colleges and the opening of the doors of white universities to Negroes who wanted to do advanced work. "Negroes must insist continually, in season and out of season, that voting is necessary to modern manhood, that color discrimination is barbarism, and that black boys need education as well as white boys.

"In failing thus to state plainly and unequivocally the legitimate demands of their people, even at the cost of opposing an honored leader [Booker T. Washington], the thinking classes of American Negroes would shirk a heavy responsibility, — a responsibility to themselves, a responsibility to the struggling masses, a responsibility to the darker races of men whose future depends so largely on this American experiment, but especially a responsibility to this nation . . ."[9]

This in 1903 was where the debate stood. Booker T. Washington thought that his workable arrangement was the best road ahead for his people. He warned: "Our greatest danger is that in the great leap from slavery to freedom we may overlook the fact that the masses of us are to live by the productions of our hands . . . we shall prosper in proportion as we learn to dignify and glorify common labor."[10] W. E. B. DuBois applauded the teaching of the mass of the Negro people to work hard and well but "so far as Mr. Washington apologizes for injustice . . . — so far as he, the South, or the Nation, does this — we must increasingly and firmly oppose them."[11] It was with this challenge that American Negroes entered the twentieth century in the land of equality.

QUESTIONS

1. How would Washington and DuBois evaluate busing Negro students to all-white schools?

2. Is economic development more important than the achievement of equal civil rights?

3. Which man was right for his day?

SUGGESTED READING

Booker T. Washington's *Up From Slavery* (New York, 1901) and W. E. B. DuBois's *Dusk or Dawn* (New York, 1968) are both available in paperback and are both classics in American autobiographical literature. DuBois derived his title from an earlier essay, "The Dawn of Freedom," in *The Souls of Black Folk,* which contains some of the finest essays in American literature. August Meier's *Negro Thought in America, 1880-1915* (Ann Arbor, 1966) is an important study of the intellectual background of the great debate between Washington and DuBois.

---

[9]*Ibid.*, p. 55.
[10]E. D. Washington, ed., *Speeches of Booker T. Washington,* pp. 32-33.
[11]DuBois, *Souls of Black Folk,* p. 59.

PART III

THE NEGRO TODAY

Introduction

Trapped as a sharecropper on small Southern farms, confronted with laws that condemned him to second class citizenship, deprived of political power, the Negro entered the twentieth century with severe handicaps. Washington and DuBois were determined, in their differing ways, that their people should not continue to live so unhappy a life in the land of equality.

In this book, it is time to turn to problems of our own day. Now Negro leaders, in the tradition of these two great men of the past, are working with their people to achieve equality for the Negro in America. Justice cannot be done in this brief introduction to the long struggle to organize this effort. It began early in the century when Dr. DuBois and a group of dedicated associates, black and white, founded the National Association for the Advancement of Colored People (NAACP). The most terrible evil they sought to halt was the lynchings. In these actions, a Negro, feared by a white community because of a crime he was alleged to have committed, was taken from his jail by a group of white people in the area and killed. Frequently, this was accompanied by tortures inflicted by men who were encouraged by a cheering crowd of onlookers. The reporters for the NAACP's famous journal, *Crisis,* risked their lives to expose these crimes and aroused the conscience of many Americans who began to see the inhumanity not only of lynchings but also of the more subtle indignities inflicted on black men all over the nation.

Negroes were moving. They began to leave their place in the South and take wage-paying jobs in the industrial North. This twentieth-century migration of millions of rural Negroes to the Northern cities is one of the great movements of people in the history of the world. During World War I, Negroes found wage-paying jobs in industries producing war-goods. They did not obtain the highest paying jobs and when layoffs came, as in the great depression of the 1930's, they were the first to suffer. But still the cities of the North — the South Chicagos and Harlems — became the Promised Land to which deprived and desperate people came hoping for a better break for themselves — and for their children.

95

Still the nation failed to provide the opportunity these people needed. The revelation at the close of World War II of the atrocities committed by the Germans on the Jews awakened some white Americans to the fact that racial inhumanity existed in America too. But the progress combatting it was still slow. During the war, President Roosevelt ordered the end of job discrimination in war industries and, just prior to the Korean War, President Truman integrated the armed forces. Finally, in 1954, Negroes, led by Thurgood Marshall* of the legal arm of the NAACP, achieved a major victory. On May 17, 1954, they won the case called *Brown v. the Board of Education.* The Supreme Court ordered that segregation in the public schools must stop. Segregation, declared the courts, caused schools to be "inherently unequal." Negroes were quick to grasp the full message. If it was unconstitutional — if it was against the stated purpose of the nation — for black men to have to endure inequality in the schools, then, similarly, it was wrong in all other pursuits of life. Negro Americans were determined to win their full freedom at last.

Two years after the Supreme Court decision, Rosa Parks was arrested in Montgomery, Alabama for refusing to get up and give her seat on a bus to a white man. Mrs. Parks was ready to start the march to freedom and so were thousands of her neighbors in Montgomery. Led by a young Baptist minister in the city, Martin Luther King, Jr., they boycotted the bus-line and walked instead of riding the buses.

Before long, they were joined by millions of Negroes in active but non-violent protest against the indignities that had oppressed them for centuries. Their struggle against overbearing resistance aroused the conscience of white Americans and out of an alliance between concerned whites and dis-satisfied blacks was born a great movement. At the peak of its success, the advocates of civil rights in the Senate were able to ride out a three-month Southern filibuster and pass the 1964 Civil Rights Act, with titles forbidding discrimination in public accommodations and employment. A year later a brutal assault on civil rights marchers in Selma, Alabama stirred Congress to pass the first effective law ensuring the Negro's right to vote. The legal barriers to equality were crumbling at last.

Though equality before the law has not been achieved in any final form, Negro leaders have begun to emphasize another aspect of civil rights — equality of social conditions. The majority of Negroes are packed in city slums where they have little chance to enjoy legal equality because they lack the education, family stability, or income to eat at desegregated restaurants, live in integrated neighborhoods, or obtain decent jobs. Indeed, conditions in the slum ghetto often are getting worse rather than better and often the effect of this environment on its inhabitants is such that their will and ability to advance themselves are retarded. Our task in this study is to examine the progress of the drive for equality in several of its recent phases and, particularly, to explore the nation's city ghettoes and ask questions about their effects on the people who live in them.

---

*Later the first black Supreme Court Justice.

chapter 1

The Court Orders School Desegregation

Introduction

Before 1954, racial segregation was legal in the land of equality. Negroes could be put in separate schools as long as the black schoolhouse was as well equipped as the white one. It seldom was. Negroes could also be barred from public parks, restaurants, theaters, and churches. They were prevented from working at jobs and from living in neighborhoods reserved for whites. Jim Crow ruled the Southland and much of the North as well.

On May 17, 1954, the Supreme Court assaulted the doctrine of racial segregation as it was applied to the public schools:

> in the field of public education the doctrine of 'separate but equal' has no place. Separate educational facilities are inherently unequal.

When Chief Justice Earl Warren removed the sanction of the law from segregation in the schools, Negroes and white civil rights workers were quick to see the chance to banish it from America altogether. For the next ten years, the civil rights movement sought to apply the logic of the Court's school decision to all Jim Crow practices, North and South.

Still the vast majority of Negro children attending separate elementary schools in 1954 graduated from high school 12 years later without seeing a white face in their classrooms. Though the Supreme Court destroyed the legal foundation for segregation, it did not end the practice of racial separation in the nation's schools.

Summerton, South Carolina

The town of Summerton in Claredon County, South Carolina, was named two centuries ago by plantation owners who sent their families there to escape the heat of the lowlands of the Santee River. Today, tobacco and cotton are the staple products of Claredon County as they have been for over a century, for the soil is still fertile. Negroes cultivate this soil as they have for centuries, earning their living as tenants or sharecroppers. Their two- or three-room cabins dot the countryside and are crowded with children. The children attend all-Negro schools in one of the county's three school districts.

Summerton itself is a pleasant town with barely 1500 residents. Older houses in the Georgian tradition imitate a style once popular on the plantation; the newer ones are ranchhouses. White children play on the green lawns, the younger ones watched by Negro maids. In the 1940's, the white residents drove cars into town to shop while Negroes traveled in horse-drawn carts. Few white faces were seen from Summerton's sidewalks on Saturday afternoons, for the population of the town, like the county, is mostly Negro.

Briggs v. Elliot

In the late 1940's, Summerton's Negro children attended the Scott Branch school. In one class, 104 youngsters were crowded into the same room. In another class, children sat in the hall while the teacher taught from the principal's office. The school had no auditorium and no facilities for teaching either science or industrial arts. Disgusted with these conditions, 107 Negro parents petitioned the board of education to equalize Summerton's Negro and white schools. The board refused to recognize any inequalities.

With the aid of National Association for the Advancement of Colored People lawyers, the parents of one child, Harry Briggs, sued R. W. Elliot of the school board. The case, *Briggs v. Elliot,* charged that the Scott Branch school was inferior and that separate schools for Negroes violated the 14th Amendment to the Constitution. The school board then admitted that the schooling Negroes received was inferior, but pled lack of funds to equalize conditions. Meanwhile, the state of South Carolina came to the rescue of Jim Crow with a state-wide school construction program financed by a sales tax.

Negro schools in Summerton were still inferior to white schools in 1954, but the differences were much less obvious. The case, *Briggs v. Elliot,* was filed again, this time solely on the grounds that separate schools violated Negro's rights guaranteed by the 14th Amendment. When a special federal court upheld segregation in Summerton, Negroes appealed the decision. The Supreme Court then agreed to review the case in conjunction with similar cases concerning school segregation in Kansas, Virginia, and Delaware. This became the famous *Brown v. Board of Education.*

Summerton's Case

Summerton's school board hired S. Emory Rogers, a hometown lawyer, to defend Elliot. With the help of two Charlestown lawyers, Rogers prepared his brief for the Supreme Court, basing it on the decision *Plessy v. Ferguson.*

> This court recognized in *Plessy v. Ferguson* that racial segregation is the result of racial feeling. But it wisely understood that segregation cannot be effectively destroyed without destroying its causes, and that those causes cannot be legislated out of existence. Neither can they be removed by court decree. We have learned by bitter and costly experience that a prohibition

upon human conduct not acceptable by the people, although perhaps a 'noble experiment,' will inevitably fail.[1]

Summerton's lawyers also contended that running the schools was by rights the state's and not the federal government's job; that the state must take local conditions into account; and that if Summerton, with a Negro population of 2800 students, integrated with a white population of under 300, whites would be heavily outnumbered by Negroes. This would cause a violent reaction on the part of whites, most likely leading to the closing of all public schools in Summerton. Since racial feelings cannot be curbed by law, as the court had recognized in *Plessy v. Ferguson,* they argued, the law must take them into account.

"Separate educational facilities inherently unequal"

Earl Warren had come to the Supreme Court as an Eisenhower appointee after serving eleven years as Republican governor of California. As a politician, Warren made few enemies; as the Chief Justice of the Supreme Court, the opinion he rendered on May 17, 1954, made him perhaps the man most hated in the South. Speaking for a unanimous court, Warren ruled on the Briggs, Brown, and three similar cases that the 1896 *Plessy v. Ferguson* doctrine of "separate but equal" need not apply to school segregation in 1954, for times had changed:

> In approaching this problem, we cannot turn the clock back to . . . 1896 when *Plessy v. Ferguson* was written. We must consider public education in the light of its full development and its present place in American life throughout the Nation. Only in this way can it be determined if segregation in public schools deprives these plaintiffs of the equal protection of the laws.[2]

In his famous opinion in *Brown v. Board of Education,* Warren declared that segregation, even if physical facilities were equal as far as measurable qualities were concerned, deprives Negro children of equal protection under the law, for segregation implies inferiority and this affects the child's motivation and ability to learn:

> To separate them [Negro students] from others of similar age and qualifications solely because of their race, generates a feeling of inferiority as to their status in the community that may affect their hearts and minds in a way unlikely ever to be undone.[3]

Warren concluded that separate schools for Negroes and whites could never be equal schools.

> We conclude that in the field of public education the doctrine of "separate but equal" has no place. *Separate educational facilities are inherently unequal* [emphasis added]. Therefore, we hold that the plaintiffs and others similarly situated for whom the actions have been brought are, by reason of the segregation complained of, deprived of the equal protection of the laws guaranteed by the Fourteenth Amendment.[4]

---

[1]John Barlow Martin, *The Deep South Says "Never"* (New York, 1957), 48-49.
[2]347 U.S. 491-92.
[3]347 U.S. 494.
[4]347 U.S. 495.

Some Questions

What would the Supreme Court's decision mean to the men and women, and, more important, to the children of the segregated South? Would it mean a "new day" for the Negro? Would it mean the collapse of segregation's walls? Would the Court require immediate integration? Would the Court accept gradual desegregation of one grade a year? Would Southerners be able to change habits and patterns of segregation ingrained for more than sixty years? Would the South obey the law? Who would enforce it? The Supreme Court of the United States had declared segregation solely on the basis of race to be against the law of the land. But how long would it be before the law would or could be enforced?

"All deliberate speed"

In the fall following the Court's momentous decision, Summerton's 2800 Negro students returned to the all-Negro Scotts Branch school, and her 300 white pupils again attended the all-white school. Nothing had changed. Meanwhile, Attorney Rogers was preparing another brief for Justice Warren in order to delay integration in Summerton. Rogers and his colleagues presented their arguments during the first week of April, 1955. Warren announced the Court's decision on May 31. In essence, the Court gave local federal courts jurisdiction in interpreting its desegregation ruling, but required "all deliberate speed" and "good faith compliance" toward integration:

> Because of their proximity to local conditions and the possible need for further hearings the courts which originally heard these cases can best perform . . . [a] judicial appraisal [of the local school board's implementation of school desegregation]. Accordingly, we — remand these cases to those courts. In fashioning and effectuating the decrees, the courts will be guided by equitable principles . . . But it should go without saying that the vitality of these constitutional principles cannot be allowed to yield because of disagreement with them . . . the Courts will require . . . a prompt and reasonable start toward full compliance — and enter such orders and decrees . . . as are necessary and proper to admit to public schools on a racially non-discriminating basis with all deliberate speed the parties to these cases. . . .[5]

In compliance with this order, the Summerton case was hastily returned to the three-man federal court in Columbia, South Carolina, which had held original jurisdiction. The court was to interpret Warren's opinion and apply it to local conditions in Summerton. Its decision, announced in July, 1955, held that the Supreme Court's ruling did not require integration; it merely outlawed forced segregation of schools while permitting voluntary segregation; that is, Negroes could enroll in all-white schools, but need not be forced to attend them if they preferred the segregated Negro school.

No Desegregation in Summerton

In September, 1955, Summerton's schools opened amidst a certain amount of expectation. Would Negroes try to enroll in the all-white school? None

---

[5]349 U.S. 299-301.

tried and nothing out of the ordinary happened. During the next several months Negroes who had signed the original desegregation petition lost their jobs or their credit in local stores. Some were forced to leave town. A church presided over by the minister who had gathered the signatures was burned to the ground. And ten years later, still nothing had happened in Summerton; Negro students continued attending Negro schools, while whites attended all-white schools. Summerton's schools as of August, 1965, were still as segregated as they were when the Supreme Court had outlawed desegregation.

In Summerton, Attorney Emory Rogers explained to reporter John Martin the reasons he and his neighbors fought integration:

> There's four, five Nigra houses in my front yard. Down here, they're all over our front yard and our back yard. Working with us, playing with our children. We can't possibly see our children in their schools. Then at about sixteen there'll be, probably, a marriage . . . But even aside from that, we can't do it. If we desegregated the schools here, it would mean twenty-five Nigra children and three white children in every classroom. I don't think your daughter would be comfortable in that situation. I know mine wouldn't.

> It goes far beyond the color of the skin, too. I wouldn't want my child to be constantly associating with Brooklyn Jews or Harlem Puerto Ricans or Mott Street Chinese. We have a little different standards and we want to bring our children up with different standards. And so do you. We segregate all the time on an economic basis, and so do you. You wouldn't want to bring your daughter up in a slum in Chicago. Neither would I. You've got to remember that less than a hundred years ago these Nigras were slaves.

> We have a culture and we intend to preserve it. It wasn't any use my telling the Supreme Court we were going to integrate because we're not. We aren't even going to make plans to integrate. We do expect to study the subject.

> We can study it. But as for integrating, not in the forseeable future. You [the North] may force this down our throats. You may force us to integrate our schools. You may send bayonets and troops down here because you think it'd take that to do it in South Carolina and Alabama and Mississippi and Georgia. But you've done that once — what good will that do the North?[6]

Little Desegregation in the Deep South

Racial attitudes in Summerton are not much different from feelings in most of the rural South. Rather than integrate its public schools as required by the courts, Prince Edward County in Virginia shut them completely in 1959 and did not reopen them until ordered to do so by the Supreme Court in 1964. During that interval white children were educated in private schools, while most of the county's Negro children attended no schools whatsoever. In 1957, violence erupted in Little Rock, Arkansas, when nine Negro students tried to attend previously all-white Central High School. Only the interference of federal troops made it possible for these students to attend school. As of May, 1965, ninety-seven percent of all black children in the Deep South attended all-Negro schools and only three percent attended schools with whites. These facts and statistics have prompted a group of 300 prominent Southern educators and clergymen to state:

---

[6]John Barlow Martin, *The Deep South Says "Never,"* pp. 70-71.

. . . In 1955, the Supreme Court adopted the rule of "all deliberate speed" in school desegregation matters. For a tragic decade much of the South has involved itself in little deliberation, less speed. Desegregation of public schools has been token.[7]

In 1957, Federal troops were used to enforce court-ordered desegregation.
(The Bettmann Archive, Inc.)

[7]"54% of Compliance Data Accepted by Federal Officials," *Southern School News,* XI (June, 1965), 3.

QUESTIONS

1. Do you agree with Chief Justice Warren that segregation deprives Negroes of equal protection because it "generates a feeling of inferiority," or with Rogers that segregation results from racial feelings "which cannot be legislated out of existence"?

2. Do you agree the courts should permit voluntary segregation rather than force desegregation?

3. Evaluate Attorney Roger's claim that segregation in the South is really no different than economic segregation in the North.

SUGGESTED READING

An excellent job of reporting white Southern attitudes and resistance to desegregation is John Barlow Martin's *The Deep South Says "Never"* (New York, 1957). This Southern view is presented also in James Jackson Kilpatrick's *The Southern Case for School Segregation* (New York, 1962). Two fine documentary collections on the 1954 Court decisions and its ramifications are Hubert Humphrey, ed., *School Desegregation: Documents and Commentaries* (New York, 1964), and Benjamin Ziegler, ed., *Desegregation and the Supreme Court* (Boston, 1958). A moving story of the attempt to integrate Central High School in Little Rock, Arkansas, is Daisy Bates' *The Long Shadow of Little Rock* (New York, 1962).

chapter 2
Public Accommodations

Introduction

On his way home from an overseas assignment an American G.I. was refused a cup of coffee at a segregated lunch counter because he was a Negro.

An American family traveling on a federal highway drove nearly 100 extra miles to find a motel that would rent them a room, because they were Negroes.

On his way from New York City to Washington, D.C., a foreign diplomat could not buy a meal at a roadside restaurant because he was a Negro.

A college professor was unable to attend the theater in her home town because she was a Negro.

Segregation and Jim Crow

These four incidents, and hundreds like them, were commonplace only a few years ago. They formed part of a pattern of racial segregation practiced openly in the South and subtly in the North. This pattern was extended to almost every aspect of race relations. Negroes working in a southern factory used rest rooms separate from those used by whites. Negroes also entered factories by separate doors, or at separate times, if they were hired at all.

In grocery stores and department stores, where Negroes were allowed to spend their money in the presence of whites, they could not use the same rest rooms, drinking fountains, or lunch counters. When traveling, Negroes sat in separate taxis, trains, buses, or in separate sections of those facilities. Special waiting rooms were built for Negroes and they could not sit in the rooms reserved for whites. Negroes had to stand before the ticket booths labeled "colored" while agents first sold fares to white customers.

Justice, too, was not color-blind. Courtrooms contained Bibles marked "white" or "colored"; Negroes were seated in back of the court room. If found guilty by a jury, which was usually all-white, the Negro defendant would be sentenced by a white judge to a segregated prison.

(Ewing Galloway)

Restaurants, hotels, motels, soda fountains, lunch counters, haberdashers, barbershops, beauty parlors, etc., were designated for one race or the other. Woe to the Negro who broke the color line and asked for service in a store catering to whites only. The only Negroes in white restaurants entered by the back door and worked in the kitchen or waited on tables.

Segregation extended also to places of amusement, for Negroes were barred from theaters, movie houses, amusement parks, swimming pools, pool halls, bowling alleys, parks, and zoos. Even when these facilities were supported by public money, that is when Negro as well as white tax money paid for them, Negroes frequently could not use them. In one town, officials removed park benches when Negroes began sitting on them.

The segregation described above was frequently required by law; state or local ordinances demanded that Negroes and whites be separated in public facilities. These Jim Crow laws covered everything from railroad trains to zoos. But much of the racial segregation was a matter of private choice — white property owners chose to exclude Negroes in deference to their white customers, in deference to local custom, or in deference to their own prejudices.

The Pattern of Segregation

Segregation in public accommodations was part and parcel of private discrimination practiced by a society which considered Negroes inferior and kept them in a place separate from and usually below that assigned to whites.

This pattern was acted out by the white gentleman who called his 40-year-old Negro porter "boy" while tipping him 25 cents for carrying his bags to the train; by the white matron who called her Negro servant "auntie," but never "Mrs."; by the white child who called Negro adults by their first name and by the Negroes themselves who addressed the young lad as "Mister"; by the Southerner who angrily asked his Northern friend whether he wanted his sister to marry a "Nigra." This pattern is seen again in the practices of paying Negroes less money for doing the same type of work performed by their white counterparts and of not promoting Negroes to positions of authority over whites. This pattern is reflected in the North by whites who worry when Negroes move into their neighborhood; by the raised eyebrow at interracial dancing; and by the strong objections to interracial marriages. Segregation in public accommodations covers only one aspect of a discriminatory pattern which has downgraded and humiliated black people for centuries. So persuasive has this pattern been that for centuries Negroes accepted the inferiority it implied.

Sit-ins in Jackson, Mississippi

Three Negro college students walked quietly down Capital Street in Jackson, Mississippi, in late May, 1963, and entered a Woolworth store. Once inside, they made their way to the all-white lunch counter and sat down, asking to be served. All but one of the white customers got up and left. The waitress closed down the counter. As store detectives watched the scene, whites began crowding around the area. The three Negroes remained at the counter. For an hour, while tension built up, there was no incident. Then whites moved in back of the Negro sit-ins and someone in the gathering crowd shouted, "Go back to Russia, you black bastards!"[1] A blonde snatched a mustard dispenser from the counter, tugged on the dress of a Negro sit-in, and squirted a thick stream of mustard down the back of her neck. Other whites grabbed catsup bottles and cups of coffee and emptied their contents on the Negroes.

A burly ex-cop pushed his way through the crowd and knocked Memphis Norman, one of the demonstrators, to the ground. As Norman lay on the floor, the former policeman repeatedly kicked him in the face and the crowd roared its approval. Norman, doing nothing to defend himself, began bleeding profusely from the mouth. Store detectives finally arrested him on a charge of disturbing the peace, and arrested the former policeman on an assault charge. Norman later was sentenced to six months in jail and fined $500, while his assailant was jailed for 30 days and fined $100.

Meanwhile, more sit-ins arrived and took seats at the lunch counter. A white college professor was punched to the floor, but regained his seat. Whites crowded in and poured salt and pepper on his wounds. Outside, policemen refused to enter the store unless asked to do so by the store's managers. The crowd, becoming more unruly, began picking up odds and

---

[1]Newsweek, June 10, 1963, LXI:23, p. 28.

ends from other sections of the store and hurling them at the demonstrators. Within fifteen minutes, the managers turned off the lights and cleared the store. The sit-in had lasted for two hours.

A History of the Sit-ins

The Negroes protesting segregated lunch counters in Jackson, Mississippi, followed the lead of their brothers in Greensboro, North Carolina, nor were the North Carolinians the first members of their race to challenge racial segregation in the South. Indeed, the first organized assault on the walls of separate facilities was made in 1947 when sixteen Negroes and whites rode in buses through Virginia and North Carolina to test a Supreme Court decision banning racial segregation in interstate busing. Members of the group were arrested several times for violating local segregation laws, but there was no violence. Two years later, Negroes challenged the segregation practices which prevented members of their race from using Palisades Amusement Park in New Jersey. The publicity gained by their demonstrations was largely responsible for New Jersey joining several other states in banning racial segregation in public accommodations. By 1964, thirty-two states had such laws on their books, but none of these states was in the South, where discrimination was so blatant.

On December 1, 1955, Mrs. Rosa Parks, a Negro, was just too tired to get up and stand in the back of the bus so a white passenger could take her seat. The driver stopped the bus and a policeman arrested Mrs. Parks. In protest, 42,000 Negroes in Montgomery, Alabama, where Mrs. Parks lived, refused to use the city's buses, many preferring to walk up to five or ten miles rather than accept the humiliation of more discrimination. The boycott lasted several months and ended with the bus company, on the verge of bankruptcy, surrendering to the demands of the boycott's leader, the late Martin Luther King, Jr. Montgomery's Negroes had finally won the right to sit in any part of the bus they chose, and no longer needed to surrender their seats when the bus became crowded.

Inspired by the Montgomery boycott, which had demonstrated what organization and determination could accomplish, Negro protest movements became more frequent, and in the 1960's were almost commonplace. While sit-in demonstrators, as in Jackson, Mississippi, challenged segregation in restaurants, freedom riders challenged interstate bus discrimination and discrimination in terminal facilities, wade-ins challenged segregation in pools, and pray-ins challenged discrimination in churches. Hardly a week went by without Negroes protesting segregation in some kind of public facility, and many of these protests were met by mass arrests, and some with violence. While the demonstrators as a rule practiced nonviolence, indignant whites did not. However, the Negro community could not restrain themselves completely and with occasional violent outbursts expressed their anger at the treatment given the demonstrators. Negroes like Martin Luther King, Jr., now openly advocated the disobeyance of all ordinances designed to perpetuate segregation, and some leaders began wondering whether Americans were losing their respect for law and order. As the crisis deepened, it became apparent that the nation must take action.

A Plea from President Kennedy

On June 11, 1963, just two weeks after the Jackson incident, President John F. Kennedy addressed his countrymen in both the North and the South:

> I hope that every American, regardless of where he lives, will stop and examine his conscience about this and other related incidents.
>
> This nation was founded by men of many nations and backgrounds. It was founded on the principle that all men are created equal, and that the rights of every man are diminished when the rights of one man are threatened.
>
> Today we are committed to a worldwide struggle to promote and protect the rights of all who wish to be free. And when Americans are sent to Vietnam or West Berlin, we do not ask for whites only. . . .
>
> It ought to be possible for American consumers of any color to receive equal service in places of public accommodations, such as hotels and restaurants, and theaters and retail stores without being forced to resort to demonstrations in the street. . . .
>
> It ought to be possible, in short, for every American to enjoy the privileges of being American without regard to his race or his color.[2]

The Request for Public Accommodations

President Kennedy's speech contained more than a plea for equal treatment — it called for congressional action on, among other things, opening public accommodations to all Americans.

> I am, therefore, asking the Congress to enact legislation giving all Americans the right to be served in facilities which are open to the public — hotels, restaurants and theaters, retail stores and similar establishments. This seems to be an elementary right.[3]

The Public Accommodations Act

The evening the President spoke, Medgar Evers, Negro leader of the Jackson demonstration, was murdered on his front doorstep. The shock of this event coupled with the impact of the demonstration hastened Congress's response to the President's call for action. Within days, bills were introduced in both House and Senate to end segregation of public facilities. The proposals underwent many modifications. In its final form, the law covered hotels, motels, lunch counters, restaurants, gasoline stations, theaters and stadiums — it specifically did not include bowling alleys and other places of recreation, barbershops, and other service establishments or retail stores. A person who suffered discrimination could file suit in a federal court; the federal government would then ask a newly created community relations service to investigate the complaint and seek voluntary compliance with the law. If the negotiations failed to bring compliance, the suit would proceed. The federal government could supply lawyers, but the individual claiming discrimination would pay court costs and his own lawyers's fees. If the government could prove the existence of a pattern of

---

[2]*Vital Speeches of the Day, XXIX* (July 1, 1963), p. 546.
[3]*Vital Speeches of the Day, XXIX* (July 1, 1963), p. 547.

discrimination in an area, it could file suits against offenders. A separate section prohibited segregation in publicly owned facilities. The law did not go as far as some civil rights demonstrators had hoped, but it went a long way toward the complete elimination of discrimination in public accommodations.

Congress Debates Public Accommodations

The final version of the Public Accommodations bill was the product of nearly thirteen months of Congressional debate, filibustering, and compromise, and it provided a hotly contested issue for the 1964 Presidential election. While it is impossible to sum up all the arguments for and against this bill, it is possible to reproduce some of the strongest arguments against it and a short debate on its merits. The arguments for the bill have already been presented in the speech by President Kennedy.

Farris Bryant, governor of Florida, presented an argument against the Public Accommodations provisions before the Senate in 1963. Governor Bryant believed the bill threatened the right of property owners to choose their customers and thus deprived them of the right to use their own property as they saw fit:

> The debate in which we are now engaged is over the assertion of a new right: the right of nonowners of property to appropriate it from the owners. The new right is asserted in the name of equality. Differently stated, this is a debate between those who seek to preserve freedom in the use of property by its owners and those who would appropriate a part of the bundle of rights which make up that ownership, without compensation, to the public, in the name of equality.

> May I suggest, gentlemen, that the proper goal for the Congress to seek is not a transfer of property rights, but freedom. We would all agree that the traveler is free and should be free not to buy. He can pass a hotel or a motel he does not like because he does not like the town, he does not like the color of the hotel, or he does not like the name. . . .

> Why not? He ought to be able to do these things. He is a free man. So is the owner of the property. And if the traveler is free not to buy because he does not like the owner's mustache, accent, prices, race, other customers, or for any or no reason, the owner of the property ought to have the same freedom. That, it seems to me, is simple justice. The wonder is really that it can be questioned.[4]

Strom Thurmond and Franklin D. Roosevelt, Jr., on Public Accommodations

Strom Thurmond, a senator from South Carolina, became so disgusted with the Democratic party's stand on civil rights that he became a Republican. Franklin D. Roosevelt, Jr., a loyal Democrat, son of the former President, and Undersecretary of Commerce, argued passionately with Thurmond at the Senate Commerce Committee hearings on the Public Accommodations bill. Thurmond, like Bryant, claimed to be championing

---

[4]U.S. Cong., *Senate Civil Rights — Public Accommodations,* Hearings before Committee on Commerce, 88 Cong., 1 Sess., pursuant to S. 1732 (Washington, 1963), pp. 919-20.

property rights. Roosevelt, like President Kennedy, claimed to be championing human rights. Excerpts of their debate quoted below should help the reader determine whether a person's right to discriminate on his own property is more important than another man's right to be served without discrimination.

Senator Thurmond: . . . I think every citizen ought to have equal rights. But as to whether they want to serve people on their private property is a matter for them. That is a freedom, isn't it? Isn't that freedom, to handle your own private property as you see fit?

Mr. Roosevelt: I look upon this from a different point of view. I believe that if a man goes into a business which holds itself out as rendering service to the general public, he has an obligation to serve the general public regardless of whether the individual be a Jew, a Catholic, a Puerto Rican, a Negro, a white, Protestant, or anything else. I think that as long as he is a citizen and comes under the constitutional rights of our country, then in my opinion — this is obviously a difference between us — I believe property rights are secondary to human rights.

Senator Thurmond: Mr. Secretary, in closing, don't you feel, down in your heart, if you really believe in the Constitution, that a man has a right to operate his business in a way that he sees fit, to close it any hour he wants to, and under your theory that you have enunciated here today, if he is forced to take anybody . . . will not that lead eventually to the Government fixing the price that he can charge, the other accommodations he will have to provide in such facility, and various other items that could arise in connection with the operation of such a business?

Mr. Roosevelt: Senator, I don't believe in scarecrows, and I think I have made my position clear, that I think that human rights come before property rights in the case of public accommodations.

Senator Thurmond: Can you have any human rights when you destroy property rights?

Mr. Roosevelt: I don't believe that we are destroying property rights. In fact, I think I tried to make clear that we are strengthening the private property rights.

Senator Thurmond: Isn't that one of the chief policies that has been followed by the Communists when they take over, is to destroy property rights, and that eventually leads to the destruction of human rights?

Mr. Roosevelt: Now, Senator, if you are trying to imply that because I support this legislation, I am on the verge of becoming a Communist, . . .

Senator Thurmond: . . . You do not think that deprivation of the use of property is a destruction of freedom?

Mr. Roosevelt: This does not deprive the individual property owner of his property. It simply requires that if he is going to hold himself out as giving service to the general public, that he give it to all the public, all citizens equally. That is all.[5]

A Major Step Forward

In July, 1964, Congress passed the Public Accommodations bill into law when it approved the Civil Rights Act of 1964. Hours later, President Johnson signed the historic measure, making it illegal to bar Negroes from

[5]Hearings on *Civil Rights — Public Accommodations*, pp. 750-51, 755-56.

public facilities because of their color. It was widely hailed as a major step forward in advancing human rights. Within seven months, the Supreme Court ratified this step by unanimously upholding the constitutionality of this section. The Court decreed that the commerce clause in the Constitution granted Congress the power to ban racial discrimination in facilities which catered to people traveling between states or received a substantial portion of its supplies from out of state. This decision came as no surprise to lawyers and constitutional experts who found ample precedent in Congress's regulation of wages and hours of employment in facilities similar to those covered by the Public Accommodations bill.

The bill was held to be entirely in keeping with the ancient English common-law tradition that any man abroad on the highway may stop at any inn and make use of its accommodations. The Negro GI, the colored family, the African diplomat, and the Negro college professor can no longer legally be denied service in restaurants, hotels, theaters, or similar establishments. Nor will Negroes be arrested for sitting at lunch counters. The right to use public facilities has been guaranteed to all Americans, though habits bred under segregation and the lack of money will still prevent many Negroes from using facilities formerly reserved for whites.

QUESTIONS

1. Was the real revolution in public accommodations the law or the change in Negroes' attitudes about themselves which would no longer permit them to accept Jim Crow?

2. Were Negroes and whites justified in breaking laws that enforced segregation?

3. When the right of a property holder to discriminate interferes with the right of a customer to equal treatment, which do you feel should be upheld?

SUGGESTED READING

Merrill Proudfoot's *Diary of a Sit-In* (Chapel Hill 1962) sensitively chronicles the day-by-day events of the Knoxville, Tennessee sit-in and places the movement in Christian perspective. James Peck's *Freedom Ride* (New York, 1962) gives an excellent personal account of the efforts to desegregate interstate bus travel. A blow-by-blow description of the Jackson, Mississippi, affair is contained in Michael Dorman's *We Shall Overcome* (New York, 1965). The title of Don Knight, ed., *Legal Aspects of the Civil Rights Movement* (Detroit, 1965) suggests its contents. It also contains a text of the 1964 Civil Rights Act.

chapter 3
The Voting Rights Act of 1965

Introduction

Surrounded by his deputies, Dallas County's Sheriff "Big Jim" Clark stood watching 200 Negroes waiting patiently on line in Selma, Alabama. The Negroes were trying to register to vote and Clark had been ordered by a federal court not to interfere. But Clark saw no reason why he need obey the court injunction when the Negroes themselves had one hundred more people on the registration line than the court allowed them.

Reports vary on what happened next. Mrs. Annie Lee Cooper, who had twice before in two years tried unsuccessfully to register, claimed that Sheriff Clark yanked her out of line, twisted her arm, and struck her on the head. Annie Cooper had lived most of her life in the North and refused to accept such treatment. She struck Clark in the eye. Three deputies seized her and pinned her down on the ground while Clark beat her over the head with his night stick. Mrs. Cooper was then led away to jail where she was held on an assault charge.

Voter Registration in Selma, Alabama

Mrs. Cooper's arrest occurred on January 25, 1965. She had been standing on line in front of the Dallas County courthouse in Selma, waiting to register. During the month that Mrs. Cooper tried unsuccessfully to register, a total of 282 Negroes had been arrested for doing the same thing. Some had waited in line for more than five hours. Only one applicant was permitted to fill out registration forms at a time. Though as many as 148 whites had filled out registration forms in a single day, only ninety-three negroes were permitted to do so that entire month. Each Negro applicant was required to complete a questionnaire asking for biographical information, to write parts of the Constitution dictated by the registrar, to define words such as "capitation," and "apportionment," and to answer parts of a twenty-page test on the United States Constitution and government. Sample questions included:

Sheriff Clark subdues Annie Lee Cooper.   *(Wide World Photos, Inc.)*

Name two things that the states are forbidden to do by the United States Constitution.

If election of the president becomes the duty of the United States House of Representatives and it fails to act, who becomes President of the United States and when?

How many votes must a person receive in order to become President if the election is decided by the United States House of Representatives?[1]

Name two rights a person has after he has been indicted by a grand jury.

Where do presidential electors cast ballots for President?[2]

The test itself, as *Time* magazine commented, was "so difficult that Chief Justice Earl Warren might well have trouble passing without a favorable nod from the registrar."[3] None of the 93 Negro applicants passed it.

The Selma March

The events following Mrs. Cooper's arrest were far more dramatic than those leading up to it. By February 5, 1965, over 2600 Negroes had been

---

[1]New York *Times,* January 31, 1965, p. 55.
[2]*Time,* LXXXIV (February 5, 1965), p. 24.
[3]*Time,* LXXXIV (January 29, 1965), p. 21.

arrested for "disturbing the peace" or "parading without a license" or "contempt of court." More than 500 prisoners were children who had joined the protest movement launched by their parents. The children were herded into the countryside with billy clubs and electric prods and then dispersed. Seven hundred adults were sent 60 miles away to a work camp. Martin Luther King, Jr., who directed the protest at Selma, was arrested and spent four days in jail because he refused to put up bail money. In a neighboring county, more than 400 Negro demonstrators were dispersed by state police and local residents. One demonstrator, Jimmie Lee Jackson, died of a wound from a shotgun fired by a state trooper.

To protest Jackson's slaying and to dramatize the Negro's desire to vote, Martin Luther King, Jr., called for a fifty mile march from Selma to the state capital in Montgomery. More than 650 Negroes and whites, carrying bedrolls and food, assembled at the Brown Street Chapel in preparation. The protest march was scheduled to cross the bridge over the Alabama River just outside of Selma and proceed along Highway 80 to Montgomery. On the other side of the bridge, 500 state troopers and Jim Clark's deputies, mounted on horseback, stood waiting. State Police Major John Cloud ordered the marchers:

> "Turn around and go back to your church! You will not be allowed to march any further! You've got two minutes to disperse!"[4]

But before the two minutes passed, Cloud spoke to his forces and the troops advanced in a solid white wall on the marchers. As the front line of

On route 80, protest marchers were violently dispersed.   *(Wide World Photos, Inc.)*

---

[4]*Time,* LXXXIV (March 19, 1965), p. 24.

demonstrators fell, policemen whipped out their billy clubs and waded further into the panicked crowd, clubbing and battering skulls while white spectators applauded and whistled. On horseback, Clark and his deputies rode into the stragglers, and troopers hauled out tear gas bombs. The violence did not stop until the last straggler was back in town and sheltered in the Brown Street Chapel. Seventy-eight marchers were hospitalized, and Selma's streets were completely cleared of Negroes.

The National Reaction

The nation was shocked by the brutality at the bridge outside of Selma. President Lyndon Johnson compared the "search for freedom" at Selma to Lexington and Concord. More than 400 clergymen and many other Northerners rushed to Selma to "bear witness" and demonstrate their sympathy with the Alabama Negroes who sought the right to vote. In Selma, a Unitarian minister from Massachusetts, the Reverend James Reeb, was clubbed to death by four assailants as he left a cafe in the company of several other clergymen. The proud march of black and white citizens from all across the nation into Montgomery from Selma demonstrated that the nation's conscience had been stirred. Finally, the federal government acted to protect the Negroes' rights to protest peaceably and to correct the grievance which prompted protest — the systematic denial of the right to vote.

The Dallas County Cases

A town of fine houses, pre-Civil War Selma, Alabama, was ideally situated in the heart of the cotton country and surrounded by thousand-acre plantations. Negroes far out-numbered Selma's white population, then as now. Except for a brief period during Reconstruction, Selma's Negroes did not enjoy many of the rights of freedom.

Dallas County is still fifty percent rural and two-thirds of the rural population is black. Median family income for Negroes in 1964 was $1393, or about one-third the state average. In Dallas County, most Negroes did not complete seventh grade. And in a county where nearly one-half of the eligible voting population was black, less than two percent were registered to vote while sixty-three percent of eligible whites were registered. In neighboring Wilcox and Lowndes County, not a single Negro was registered.

In 1957, Congress passed the first federal voting rights bill since Reconstruction. It authorized the attorney general to bring suits to prohibit discrimination in state and federal elections and to prohibit intimidation of voters by state officials or private citizens. But the act did not permit the attorney general to inspect the registration records of Southern counties in order to prove discrimination. A Civil Rights Act, passed in 1960, corrected this weakness, and in 1961, the Department of Justice instituted its first suit under the new law. The suit charged Selma's voting registrar with systematically discriminating against Negroes. The trial lasted thirteen months. It took another six months for the court to hand down its decision. Yes, there had been discrimination in the past, the court admitted. But since this discrimination supposedly had stopped, the court refused to order Selma's voting registrars to allow Negroes to register.

The United States Government appealed this decision and finally obtained the order against discrimination which it sought. The registrars replied by raising registration requirements for both races. This would have the effect of "freezing" the current registration of sixty-three percent of all whites and less than two percent of all Negroes. In February, 1964, the Alabama legislature made the more difficult standards state-wide by instituting the test described earlier. The United States government again went to court and on February 4, 1965, obtained an order requiring Dallas County to use easier tests to register Negroes. But registration facilities need be open only two days a month — and with delaying tactics it could take years to register all of Dallas County's 14,000 blacks. Ultimately, the court ordered the appointment of federal registration officials as provided under the Civil Rights Act of 1964.

In the meantime the Student Nonviolent Coordinating Committee (SNCC), under the leadership of John Lewis, launched a voter registration campaign in Selma. At the same time, Sheriff Jim Clark launched a campaign of harrassment and arrests for SNCC workers. The climax of the campaign was the confrontation on Highway 80. The day that Clark and the state troopers put seventy-eight demonstrators in the hospital, a total of only 383 Negroes were on the Dallas County voting rolls, despite four years of litigation by the federal government. This number was only greater by 171 than the number of Negroes registered in 1956, the year before the first voter registration act was passed. Indeed, little progress had been made in Selma, Dallas County, Alabama.

Katzenbach Testifies

It was Attorney General Nicholas Katzenbach's job to prosecute violators of the nation's voting rights laws. His frustration in obtaining favorable judgments, as in the Dallas County cases, is explained below in his own words:

> I could cite numerous examples of the almost incredible amount of time our attorneys must devote to each of the 71 voting rights cases filed under the Civil Rights Acts of 1957, 1960, and 1964. It has become routine to spend as much as 6,000 man-hours only in analyzing the voting records in a single county — to say nothing of preparation for trial and the almost inevitable appeal.
>
> I could cite numerous examples of how delay and evasion have made it necessary for us to gauge judicial relief not in terms of months, but in terms of years. For the fact is that those who are determined to resist are able, even after apparent defeat in the courts, to devise whole new methods of discrimination. And often that means beginning the whole weary process all over again.[5]

---

[5]U.S. Cong., Senate, *Voting Rights,* Hearings before subcommittee No. 5 of the Committee on the Judiciary, 89 Cong., 1 Sess., pursuant to H.R. 6400 (Washington, 1965), p. 5.

President Johnson Asks for a More Effective Law

On March 15, 1965, a week and a day after the attacks on demonstrators at Selma, President Lyndon Johnson addressed a joint session of Congress and the nation:

> Many of the issues of civil rights are very complex and most difficult. But about this there can and should be no argument! Every American citizen must have an equal right to vote.
>
> There is no reason that can excuse the denial of that right. There is no duty which weighs more heavily on us than the duty we have to insure that right.[6]

Even before his speech, the President had consulted with Negro leader Martin Luther King, Jr., Republican leader Senator Everett McKinley Dirksen, and Attorney General Nicholas Katzenbach. The outline of a bill was drawn and presented by the President in his speech, and Congressional leadership gave a quick command to the House Judiciary Committee to begin consideration immediately. Out of this ferment emerged the Voting Rights Act of 1965, which the President signed into law in August.

The Voting Rights Act of 1965

The Voting Rights Act is directed at states and counties which, in the past, have systematically denied Negroes the right to vote. It applies only to counties and states where fifty percent of the voting age population is not registered to vote or did not vote in the last presidential election, and had, as of November 1, 1964, a literacy test or other device to determine qualification of voters. This provision would apply to the states of Alabama, Alaska, Georgia, Louisiana, Mississippi, South Carolina, and Virginia, to thirty-four counties in North Carolina, and to one county in each of three other states. In these areas, the literacy tests and other qualifying devices are automatically suspended unless the state can prove to a federal court that there has been no discrimination over the past ten years. To these areas, the Attorney General may send federal examiners to register anyone who meets state age and residency requirements. These examiners are to be employees of the United States Civil Service Bureau. They may be sent in an area at the discretion of the Attorney General or when the Attorney General receives more than 19 complaints of voter discrimination from that district. The federal examiners will register applicants without requiring any kind of literacy or moral character test, devices which have traditionally been used to bar qualified Negroes from voting.

Objections to the Voting Rights Act

Northern Republicans and Democrats alike supported the Voting Rights Act so overwhelmingly that Southern senators did not filibuster. Nevertheless, there were some important criticisms leveled at the measure. Some thought it unconstitutional even though the Attorney General had written it with the 15th Amendment specifically in mind. Others thought it punitive

---

[6]New York *Times*, March 16, p. 30.

— punishing the South for what it had done in the past, though President Johnson argued that the South need merely not discriminate and there would be no problem. And some worried about the effect of permitting semi-literate Negroes to vote, though these people had never worried about Southerners preventing literate Negroes from voting. One of the most vehement statements against the Voting Rights Act was made by W. B. Hicks, a member of an organization called the Liberty Lobby. Hicks concentrated his attack on what he believed were the punitive aspects of the law, and the effect of allowing illiterate Negroes to vote:

> The President's law is punitive. It is designed to punish the South for what it has done for nearly 100 years in semilegal contravention of the 15th amendment — . . .

> The punishment contemplated is more than severe — it is a death sentence. For the next ten years, this law forbids the poorest and least educated part of the Nation to use any qualifications for voting other than age and residence. The result of this punishment can be seen as clearly as if it had already happened.

> First, the rise of a new class of Southern State politican — a breed of demagogues — coming into political power on a wave of pie-in-the-sky promises of free State money for everyone.

> Next, the futile attempts to carry out those promises by taxing the farms, business, and industry of the South at ever-increasing rates, even while failing to satisfy the demands of the poor for more and more and more and more. Then, the flight of business and industry from the unbearable demands of the welfare state, and the tragic streams of white refugees — following their jobs to the North and West. . . .

> Let there be no question about it. If the President's law is passed, the South will disappear from the civilized world just as surely and certainly as did Haiti in 1804. Under the terms of this punitive law, the South will be sentenced to government by its least capable inhabitants for ten long years. No civilization so governed has ever survived and there is no reason to believe that this one will. . . .

> Even granting that the South has sinned, as so many believe, by trying to have its cake and eat it too — by using literacy tests to restrict the Negro vote while letting whites vote without restriction — did we not all help establish the pattern for the South — never insisting, until now, that the South make the hard decision — the decision to apply the same necessary standards to whites as well as blacks?

> Now, are we to give the South no opportunity to choose; to do the thing that is necessary to its own survival, as well as ours? Are we to pass a law or a death sentence?[7]

Impact of the Negro Vote

The Voting Rights Act, ironically, was passed almost too late to help most Negroes in the South. In only seven Southern counties and in no Southern states are Negroes in the majority, so even when and if all Negroes are registered, their votes will not give them control over their own destinies. Nevertheless (by July, 1968) some changes have been effected

---

[7]Hearings on *Voting Rights,* pp. 534-35.

by the law. A Negro sheriff was elected in Tuskegee, Alabama, as were Negro legislators in other Southern states. The Alabama Democratic party dropped its white supremacist label, and some white politicians have become aware of the wishes of their black constituents. To some degree, there has been a reaffirmation of faith by blacks and whites in the democratic process.

QUESTIONS

1. In your judgment, why were Southerners more afraid of giving literate Negroes the right to vote than illiterate whites?

2. Should Clark, rather than King, have been jailed for his part in the demonstrations in Selma?

3. On the basis of Selma's and Alabama's resistence to Negro voting was the denial of state control over registration justified?

SUGGESTED READING

The March 19 and 22, 1965, issues of *Time* and *Newsweek* magazines, respectively, contain excellent articles on the Selma affair. The *New York Times Sunday Magazine,* May 30, 1965, tells the story of Selma after the demonstrators went home. President Johnson's two speeches on the right to vote are among his more eloquent. The August 6 speech may be found in *Vital Speeches of the Day,* August 15, 1965.

chapter 4
Discrimination in Employment

We must not continue to ignore the terrible degradation suffered by those who are victims of discrimination in employment because of race, color, religion, and national ancestry, for this anguish is visited upon their children and continues on and on. All hope is killed in the very young; they know that although they have a high degree of intelligence, are ambitious and industrious, there is no point in pursuing higher education or looking for jobs which are commensurate with their abilities; they are not given such jobs; they know that they will be denied advancement to which they are entitled in any jobs they hold, because they are of a minority group.[1]

Representative Jacob Gilbert of New York

A Case of Discrimination

On April 30, 1964, four plumbers reported to work on a municipal project in New York City. The union plumbers, already on the job, promptly quit work. "Animals don't mix;" one plumber murmured, "why should people have to?"[2] One of the four new plumbers was a Negro, the others were Puerto Ricans. Race, the white workers argued, had nothing to do with the walkout; the new workers were not members of the union.

George Meany, president of the AFL-CIO, lent his support to the walk-out: "This union won't work with nonunion men."[3] New York Mayor Robert Wagner entered the dispute, and weeks of negotiation followed while work on the project was halted. The union finally agreed to give the four plumbers a special membership test administered by impartial observers. All four of the new plumbers failed the test.

"The disadvantage suffered by the average Negro in this country because of the color of his skin," *The New York Times* editorialized, "is no-where more burdensome than in the area of job opportunity." The plumbers' case illustrates this point. Although New York City's Negroes

---

[1]U.S. Cong., House, *Equal Employment Opportunity,* Hearings before Committee on Education and Labor, 88 Cong., 1 Sess., pursuant to H.R. (Washington, 1963), p. 49.

[2]"Unions Feel Growing Pressure to Take More Negroes", *U.S. News and World Report,* LVI (May 25, 1964), p. 88.

[3]"Unions Feel Growing Pressure to Take More Negroes", p. 88.

form thirteen percent of the town's population, they hold less than two percent of all construction jobs. In its seventy-five-year history, Local 28 of the Sheet Metal Workers International never admitted a Negro. All 3200 members of another union were white. Whites are not willing to surrender their monopoly of jobs in construction. "I'm no Rockefeller," one worker lamented, "I've got no fortune or no business to leave to my son; what's so bad if I get him first crack at an apprentice's job?"[4] During ten years of nearly continuous agitation over civil rights issues (1953-63), Negroes in New York gained only an additional quarter of one percent of the city's construction jobs.

Negroes and Employment

Job discrimination was by no means limited to New York City:

Item: Employment agencies in New Jersey were found coding job applications so Negroes can be identified and denied interviews.

Item: An ambitious and intelligent young Negro is denied a promotion because this would put him in the position of supervising white workers.

Item: A large metropolitan school system has not hired a single Negro school teacher.

Item: The manufacturer of a popular brand of aluminum cookware refuses to hire Negro salesmen.

Item: For nearly a quarter of a century, the unemployment rate among Negroes has been twice that suffered by whites. Among younger workers, Negroes have been subjected to nearly three times the rate of white unemployment.

Item: Income among Negroes is scarcely fifty-four percent of white income.

300 Years of Job Discrimination

Negroes have long experienced discrimination in employment. First as slaves and later as sharecroppers or tenant farmers, Negroes have been denied the education and opportunity to obtain decent jobs. During the pre-Civil War period most Southern states prohibited persons from teaching Negroes to read or write. Few Negroes were taught anything but the most simple agricultural tasks. After Reconstruction, poverty and racial discrimination combined to prevent most Negroes from acquiring adequate job skills. This sad fact was no less true in the North than in the South:

> There are no colored artisans in New York [in 1900]. The trade unions would prevent any such from receiving employment.[5]

During the 1920's and 1930's all of New York City's colored construction workers were required to join a union located in Harlem and limited to performing work in that part of the city. Since there was no work to be had in Harlem, the union's members decreased from 440 in 1926 to 65 in 1935. At the outbreak of World War II, in 1941, the Bureau of

---

[4]A. H. Raskin, "Civil Rights: The Law and the Unions", *The Reporter,* XXXI (September 10, 1964), p. 27.

[5]Quoted in New York State Commission Against Discrimination, *Apprentices, Skilled Craftsmen and the Negro: An Analysis.* (New York, 1960), p. 34.

Employment Security reported that:

> ... even in industries in which Negroes have by custom been accepted, many establishments which have employed Negroes in the past were refusing to employ Negroes for skilled and semi-skilled work.[6]

In the South, where the number of skilled Negro craftsmen dropped significantly between 1910 and 1940, the story was no different.

Fair Employment Practice and Its Effect

During World War II, Negroes threatened to demonstrate against defense industries' preferential hiring policies. Their agitation led to an executive order banning discrimination in the defense industry. To implement this order, President Roosevelt established the Fair Employment Practice Committee. The committee lasted for five years and was abolished in 1946. Since that time numerous executive orders have attempted to prohibit discrimination in work done under contract with the federal government. Many Northern states (twenty-five by 1964) passed their own fair employment practice laws prohibiting racial or religious discrimination in hiring, firing, and promoting. But like so many laws dealing with the racial question, their effects were slight.

The occupations which have traditionally been open to Negroes are jobs which involve unskilled labor. These have been disappearing rapidly with the introduction of machines that replace unskilled labor. New jobs are continuously opening, but Negroes cannot surmount the twin obstacles of inadequate education and racial discrimination. They have been systematically excluded from unions' apprenticeship programs.

Equal Employment Opportunities

When President Kennedy proposed the Civil Rights Act in 1963, one of its provisions was the barring of racial discrimination in employment. The bill would cover industries affecting interstate commerce that (by July, 1968) employed more than twenty-five workers. The bill would cover discrimination in hiring, firing, and promotions and would extend to exclusions or expulsions from training programs. Individuals claiming discrimination would have up to ninety days to file their complaints with the Equal Opportunities Commission established by this act. The Commission itself could file complaints on behalf of individuals, and it could also act to achieve compliance with the law through mediation and conciliation. If efforts at achieving voluntary compliance failed, however, the Commission could recommend that the Attorney General file suit against the employer in federal court.

These employment provisions in Title VII of the Civil Rights Act of 1964 were strongly contested. Alabama's Senator Lister Hill believed the bill would give preference rather than equal opportunities to Negroes. This preferential treatment for Negro minorities, Hill contended, would deny employment opportunities for white majorities. Hill argued that this

---

[6]Quoted in *Apprentices, Skilled Craftsmen and the Negro: An Analysis,* pp. 38-39.

was the wrong approach to the racial problem because it was based on expedience and emotions, rather than on education and understanding. Laws based on expedience and emotions, he maintained, invited chaos and violence. Try the South's approach to racial problems, Hill counseled his countrymen, for it is based on hundreds of years of experience.

Senator Hill Against the Equal Employment Opportunities Section

> I continue to believe in the American system of free enterprise, in the principles on which it was founded, in the right of an employer to select his employees, to promote them for merit and to discharge them for unsatisfactory performance, and because I so strongly believe these things and that they have always been a part of our American way of life, I am opposed to Title VII.
>
> It contains the weapons for the destruction of many civil and natural rights which the people of this country have enjoyed since its founding. It is based on the thesis that the best way to grant special privileges to a particular group is to deny the majority the rights they already possess. In the name of "equal employment opportunity" it seeks to establish a preference and a special "right" to employment based on "race, color, religion, or national origin."
>
> The rules and regulations of the Equal Employment Opportunity Commission . . . could compel employers to re-employ dismissed employees and to employ rejected applicants who were considered incapable and unfit. The practices of the Equal Employment Opportunity Commission would destroy the merit system as a basis for employment, upgrading, demotion, or transfer, and layoff or termination. Take for example an employer who employs fifty men. Ten of these employees can be identified with a minority group. If the employer has to lay off eight men, he would be less likely to discharge any of the ten men who could claim discrimination — whether it existed or not — and file charges with the Equal Employment Opportunity Commission, causing him harassment, expense and possible punishment. We can easily see the resulting damage to the efficiency of management and to the morale and productivity of the workers in that plant.[7]

But Senator Lister Hill's rhetoric was not enough to defeat the employment section of the Civil Rights Act of 1964, and when President Johnson signed the historic measure into law, Title VII barred racial discrimination in employment. One of the first cases to arise under the employment provisions perhaps illustrates what Senator Hill meant when he complained of "special privileges to a particular group," but the case also can be interpreted as an attempt to correct what Representative Gilbert had called the "terrible degradation suffered by those who are victims of discrimination in employment." The case dealt with alleged discrimination on a federally financed project in St. Louis, Missouri, and it is worth examining.

Discrimination and the Gateway Arch

The Gateway Arch is a 630-foot monument towering above St. Louis, Missouri. Built with federal funds, the arch memorializes the thousands of pioneers who poured through St. Louis on their way West. On January 7, 1966, a plumber and two helpers reported to work at the construction site of the Arch. No sooner had the new workers arrived at their jobs then members of five local unions walked off the project, supposedly protesting

---

[7] Lister Hill, *Speech of Senator Lister Hill In Opposition to H.R. 7152 "The Civil Rights Act of 1963"* (mimeographed copy, 1963), pp. 44-46.

the hiring of men who accept subunion standard wages. All three new workers were Negroes. Four of the unions staging the walk-out represented 5000 workers, including only three Negroes.

The air was immediately filled with charges and countercharges. The unions pointed out that the government was practicing discrimination. After all, a Negro contracter had been hired to install plumbing although a white contractor had offered to do the job for less. The government countered that it ordered the hiring of Negroes to enforce an executive ban on discrimination on the project.

The government charged that the walkout was staged to "prevent and discourage the employment on construction projects in the St. Louis area of plumbers who are members of nondiscriminating unions"[8] and that the building trade unions practicing discrimination "control virtually all the employment opportunities for these trades in the St. Louis area."[9]

The employment section of the 1964 Civil Rights Act requires thirty days of seeking voluntary compliance. After the period expired, the Justice Department filed its first "pattern of discrimination" suit. The refusal to work with the Negro plumbers was held illegal and an order was issued for the white unions to resume work. One of the unions named in the suit, the Pipefitters Local No. 562, has hired ten Negroes for special on-the-job training as part of a crash program to equalize employment opportunities and incidentally find employment in federal projects. These ten men are Local No. 562's only Negro members.

QUESTIONS

1. It has been said that equality of economic opportunity must precede all other forms of equality. Do you agree?

2. Should Negroes be given special considerations in employment because of previous discrimination in jobs, schooling, etc.?

3. Contrast the factors causing the two walk-outs described in this chapter and the solutions to the two disputes. Which solution is more in keeping with what you believe is true equality of employment opportunity?

SUGGESTED READING

Paul N. Norgen and Samuel E. Hill examine experiences under state, local, and federal fair employment practice commissions and recommend provisions for Federal FEP laws in *Toward Fair Employment* (New York, 1964). Herman Miller presents a pessimistic assessment of ghetto Negroes' employment prospects in "The Job Gap," *New York Times Magazine,* May 8, 1966. Herbert R. Northrup and Richard L. Rowan, editors of *The Negro and Employment Opportunity* (Ann Arbor, 1965), offer a comprehensive survey of all aspects of this problem by experts in the employment field.

---

[8]New York *Times,* February 5, 1966, p. 13.
[9]Earl Gottshalk, "Suit Against the Unions", *The New Republic,* CLIV (March 12, 1966), p. 8.

chapter 5

The City Slum

Introduction

As slaves, most Negroes lived in the South. They generally remained in the South during the Reconstruction period, settling on small farms and tilling the land as sharecroppers, laborers, and tenants. Before 1900, the Negroes' movement North was not massive, but thereafter the great Northern migration began. Many came to work in war industries during World War I. When America closed its gates to foreign immigrants in the 1920's, Southern Negroes helped fill the demand for cheap factory labor. The agricultural depression of the 1930's propelled Negroes off their farms and the pace of migration accelerated during World War II and afterwards. In ever-increasing numbers, Negroes left their homes in Clarendon County, South Carolina, and Selma, Alabama; they left the cotton fields and their kinfolks, their small shacks, and their jobs as tenants, sharecroppers, and farm laborers, and crowded into the big city slums of the North. In 1910, seventy-three percent of the black population lived in rural areas. By 1960, seventy-three percent lived in cities and towns.

Tragically, this great Negro migration failed to substantially improve the lot of the immigrant. Negroes, fleeing the degradation and poverty of the Southern farm, often found crowded squalor in the Northern city where open segregation was replaced by subtle forms of discrimination, helping to isolate them in crowded housing. As one Harlem resident, Claude Brown, told it:

> It seems that Cousin Willie, in his lying haste, had neglected to tell the folks down home about one of the most important aspects of the promised land: it was a slum ghetto. There was a tremendous difference in the way life was lived up North. There were too many people full of hate and bitterness crowded into a dirty, stinky, uncared-for closet-size section of a great city. Before the soreness of the cotton fields had left Mama's back, her knees were getting sore from scrubbing "Goldberg's" floor. Nevertheless, she was better off; she had gone from the fire into the frying pan.
>
> The children of these disillusioned colored pioneers inherited the total lot of their parents — the disappointments, the anger. To add to their misery, they

125

In the slum ghetto, anything may be the playground.   *(Magnum Photos, Inc.)*

had little hope of deliverance. For where does one run to when he's already in the promised land?[1]

New Haven, Connecticut

Large numbers of Negroes first migrated northward to New Haven, Connecticut, after World War II. Before the Civil War, New Haven had

---

[1]Claude Brown, *Manchild in the Promised Land* (New York, 1966), viii.

been a center for abolitionist controversies. Like many Northern cities in those days, New Haven harbored a small population of free Negroes who had their own churches and worked actively for their rights. As late as 1940, New Haven's Negro population amounted to only 6000, about seven percent of the city's population.

The Negro migration reached New Haven in the late 1950's. By 1965 one-quarter of New Haven's residents were Negroes, many from the rural South. The new arrivals were resented by older residents of both races. Almost one-half were jammed into an area covering but one-twentieth of the city's living space. Like many Northern cities, New Haven now had its own ghetto with the characteristics of all slums: poor people, dilapidated houses, and a self-perpetuating cycle of despair.

John Randolph in New Haven: the Street

John Randolph grew up in New Haven's Oak Street slum during the 1950's.[*] The house in which he lived for the first ten years of his life stood near the corner of Kilder Alley and Lafayette Street. It was a three-floor, wood-frame house, the bottom story serving as a second-hand furniture store. Four families shared the top two floors. One bathroom graced the hall and was used by all tenants. Weeds grew in the back yard and a garage connected to the house was used for raising chickens. Garbage cans were lined along the back-yard, but garbage and junk were strewn all around. The other homes in the neighborhood looked much the same: two- or three-story houses with littered yards and peeling paint; in each, four to eight families were crowded. The neighborhood stretched for blocks. It offered few opportunities for recreation for youngsters growing up in the area.

> We did crazy things when we were kids. There was no community center, no place for us to be except the streets. I remember a friend of mine when we were about six — we used to stand on the roof over the garage and throw firecrackers at the bums sleeping in the alley below.
>
> We saw a lady hit a man in the head with an axe and she busted his skull. There was blood all around. We thought for sure he was dead. We ran off the roof and told the police. But the cop paid no attention to us. That night I was in bed. There was a lot of confusion down in the street. They had found this guy where the lady hit him. The cops wanted to know if I was the kid who had seen the guy get hit. But I was just beginning to see why the general rule in my neighborhood was that you don't tell the police anything. I was scared, but I said "no." I started to cry.
>
> It ended up that they arrested a woman who had been sitting on the steps at my house when the guy was hit. We knew this lady didn't do it, but we didn't go to the police station to tell the cops. There was enough trouble in my neighborhood. People were always going to jail. There was no use to look for more trouble. No one will tell the cops anything if they can help it.[2]

---

[*]John Randolph's story is based on actual interviews; only the name has been changed.

[2]Interview with a New Haven youngster, July, 1966.

A Part of a Group

John's family lived in three rooms and the toilet was out in the hall. He had five brothers and sisters and they were close in age. Most of them slept in one room sharing bunkbeds, and one baby slept in a bassinette. The youngest child slept in a room with her mother. John's father usually was not home, and when he was home, he usually was not sober. Mrs. Randolph worked, and the children were generally left to shift for themselves. With little parental guidance, they learned that their true friends were the buddies they found outside the home.

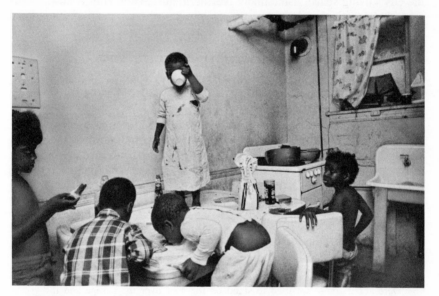

Housing in the slum ghetto — crowded and deteriorated.

(New Haven Redevelopment Agency)

Slum kids in most cases will tend to stick together no matter what. You always stick with your best friend. You always take your problems to the fellows. I guess that's because even if they can't help you, they can understand, because they are a part of it.

I was always part of a group. We had no one else to cling to. We swung in groups for protection, for kicks, for friends and for girls. You stuck with your group no matter what. We were always close; always headed in the wrong direction. But no matter what the fellows did, you always would back their play. You didn't have anyone else.[3]

The School

John's father was born in South Carolina. He had finished eighth grade and then worked the cotton fields for several years. He went into the Army in 1941, and when he came out, he decided that he could not take the life in the South. So he moved to New Haven and married a girl from the Oak

---

[3]Interview.

Street section. They had six children in the next eight years. Randolph worked on the railroad; his wife was a waitress. There were few opportunities for Negroes with educations in the 1940's and 50's, so the Randolphs saw little reason why their children should finish school. Their children saw even fewer reasons.

Last few weeks of school in seventh grade me and the fellows skipped a lot. We were only allowed to be absent about twenty days, but we didn't care. They couldn't call home when we were out of school because we didn't have a phone. Anyway, my mother was always working. The teachers never went to your home because it was dirty or because they were too lazy. Anyway, the teachers at school didn't care for Negroes.

I remember one time I was cutting up in class. The teacher said, 'John, be quiet or I'll give you an "F" for citizenship.' I says, 'Give me a double "F".' She told me to go to the office. I says, 'Hell, I ain't going to no office — I'm going home,' and I left. They didn't call my home because, like I said, we didn't have a phone and anyway my mother works.

We wanted things you could cling to. We all wanted to better ourselves. I mean making it in a slum isn't like making it in another neighborhood. We wanted things you could touch: clothes, money, a car and an apartment. School wasn't giving us that. They were giving us what they call a formal education. We didn't feel that was worth anything to us.

Fellows I knew used to quit school when they were in tenth grade. You'd be hanging around and a friend would say, 'I've got a good slave [job]! Come the weekend and he has the money. He has a good jacket on. He'd say, 'I think I'll go to the city [New York].' And you can't go to the city, you don't have a dime. All you have is a pad of assignments. Pretty soon you say, 'Why should I go to school.'[4]

Tough Enough and Clever Enough

When John was twelve his parents moved into a public housing project on Dixwell Avenue. His parents now had six rooms, but there were thirteen people sharing these rooms. Besides his parents and five brothers and sisters, there was a grandmother, an aunt, the two illegitimate children of one sister, and the husband of another. His brother-in-law was supporting a forty dollar-a-day dope habit. Within those crowded walls, life was fiercely competitive. John learned early in life to shout to be heard and to be cunning to get his way; that life was a fierce struggle for survival, and that life's rewards were the satisfactions he received from winning in this competition — that adult pleasures of liquor, sex, and dope went to those who were tough enough and clever enough to take them. He learned that in order to get these he had to beat someone else and he had to have money; and the way to win was not always the honest way:

You always think of beating someone else to make you feel better. When we sold papers in the morning before school we figured if we stayed out late then we couldn't go to school. We might make $5 a week this way and miss school a couple of mornings each week. Collection day was always on Monday the following week. Some guy would come in a big car and we'd give him the money for the week before. Only we'd spend the money before collection and figure we'd make enough the next week to pay the guy. When

---

[4]Interview.

I quit papers, I was a couple of dollars behind and I couldn't pay the guy collecting money. I was scared he'd come after me to get it. But a couple of weeks later he was arrested for embezzling $10,000. So I never had to pay him the money I owed him.

When I was about fifteen, I started hanging out with the fellows. Seems like every group I'd hang around with we'd get into worse trouble. Anyway, there was this one time we robbed this store, Jack's Mart on Ferry Street. We took forty-two blank pistols, a pellet gun and a real gun. After that we figured we were pro's. We started hanging around with these girls we swung with at the time. There was one liquor store we'd break into about once a month, and grab us a couple of cases of wine, beer and scotch. I remember one time we'd put the stuff in one of those shopping carts and wheel it right home in the shopping cart. Nobody bothered us. The girls would go to the stores downtown with these big purses and grab anything they could. When we'd get back to the house — this guy's sister would let us use a room at her house — we'd have a real party. The girls would love to drink wine. We'd all get high and really have ourselves a time. . . .

One of these guy's girl friends became pregnant. He married the chick. That was a square act. We cut him loose.[5]

A New Life

Before John was sixteen his gang was broken up. The police had discovered several hundred dollars worth of stolen goods at a friend's house. The gang was taken to juvenile court. John spent seven days in the children's building. One boy was sent to reform school in Meriden, Connecticut, for nine months. He came back an addict and is still on drugs. Another was sent to live with relatives in Puerto Rico; another to relatives in Philadelphia. The rest decided they had better not get caught again. John's father warned him he would not help him out of jail, but this was not the first time that John heard that warning. When the gang got back together it was not "the same anymore."

But something even more dramatic made John decide he would keep out of trouble. Someone took an interest in John and got him interested in doing something for his community:

A friend of mine was hanging out one night, kicking around with nothing to do and one of CPI's [Community Progress Incorporated] community workers called to him and asked if he'd do a favor and I came along too. He [the community worker] told us he wanted us to participate in a group discussion about teenagers in the community and express what we felt was necessary as far as youth programs and activities were concerned — you know, what was needed. To clear you up a bit there had been programs but there was a lack of interest in them and they wanted us to tell them why. CPI workers weren't communicating with the people they were supposed to help. After the tape [the discussion was recorded] we met the leader and we were told everyone was thrilled with the tape, and we had done a great job. We were asked to meet at the school again. We were asked if we wanted to form a club and we were kicking ideas around. We decided we'd have this club. It turned out to be a club that was really needed in the community and it was looked up to by social workers, teachers, and principals. We had no trouble getting funds or facilities or anything. Most of the boys in the club the first year were

---

[5]Interview.

what you call juvenile delinquents; all had been in trouble one time or another; some were dropouts — but all got together and really worked. We laid the foundation for the club the first year. . . .

When I got involved in this club I began to steer the rest of my friends into it because you always try to help your friends in a slum neighborhood. Even while I was in this club I got arrested a couple of times, but I found that the crimes were always lesser. . . .

We wanted to do something for the community that was really worth while. We started this big brothers club. There were some students at Yale already doing this but it was our community and we felt we should start one: go to the movies on rainy days, possibly camps free of charge. We started by taking kids to camp. It cost us about $60 to take thirty kids out. And by doing this we established a very good name in the community. Whenever anything was happening in the community, they always asked our club to be there.

We were trying with all our hearts in doing something for the community and at the same time for ourselves.[6]

In Perspective

Is John's story typical? Yes, for many white boys and many more who are black and caught in the vise of poverty that grips the ghetto. Although not all or even many Negro children steal, drink, or get into trouble, far too many live in an environment that encourages this type of behavior. Ghetto youngsters find it difficult to distinguish good from bad according to the conventions of middle-class society. The widely advertised material goals of that society seem obtainable to these children only by dishonest means. Far too few slum dwellers know a social worker who is able, as in John's case, to assist them in helping themselves out of the conditions typical of the ghetto. Though Negroes constituted only ten percent of the nation's population, they accounted for more than fifty percent of the arrests in 1963; three times as many Negro children as non-Negroes come from broken homes; and almost eight times as many Negro children are illegitimate.[7] Until life in the ghetto is changed, these facts will probably remain unchanged.

QUESTIONS

1. Explain the statistics on Negro crime and morality in terms of John's life.

2. To what extent, if any, is John responsible for the attitudes he forms about school, competition, and getting ahead? Who is responsible?

3. Is it white society's obligation to change the outlook and values of people like John Randolph?

---

[6]Interview.
[7]Office of Policy Planning and Research, United States Department of Labor, *The Negro Family: The Case for National Action* (Washington, 1965).

SUGGESTED READING

Recent accounts of Negro life in the slums are Claude Brown's autobiographical *Manchild in the Promised Land* (New York, 1965), Warren Miller's novel, *The Cool World* (Greenwich, 1967), and Kenneth Clark's sociological *Dark Ghetto* (New York, 1965). Though less recent, Richard Wright's *Native Son* (New York, 1940) is still powerful. Lee Rainwater's "The Crucible of Identity: The Lower Class Negro Family," *Daedalus* (Winter, 1966), examines the effects of the ghetto on the Negro family. A Puerto Rican in the ghetto is portrayed in Piri Thomas's *Down These Mean Streets* (New York, 1967).

chapter 6

Housing in the Suburbs
and the Cities

A Home in the Suburbs

Katherine W. is a professional social worker; her husband John teaches and coaches in New Haven. The couple was married in 1961 and shortly afterwards decided they wished to live in their own home in a suburb of New Haven. Since they had ample savings and a good income, this should not have created a great problem. But the W.'s ran into a good deal of trouble finding a home in the suburbs. Mrs. W. tells the story:

> I found some houses in the "Home" section of the paper, and I called the realtors. One of the most interesting sessions was with the Blank Agency. We had a long and pleasant chat over the phone and the salesman asked me a few questions, "where my husband worked", "what I did," and so on. We talked about his son-in-law who had worked in my office and whom I knew. It was all extremely pleasant. Then we made this appointment for him to take me to look at houses after work.

> The secretary told me he was there and I went out to meet him. He was this great big man and he turned beet-red when he saw me. When I got into his car he said, "I can't show you those houses. This is the first time I realized you were colored." I said, "What difference does that make?" and he said, "They don't want you there." I said, "Those homes are in our price range and a lot of my husband's friends live in that area." He said the owners wouldn't sell to Negroes and that he wouldn't take any Negro clients to see the houses. By this time we had driven quite a way, and he wanted to let me out on the spot, but asked him to take me back to my car. We drove back in silence.[1]

Mrs. W. reported the incident to the Connecticut Civil Rights Commission, but at that time there was no law under which they could act, and nothing was done.

As the W.'s continued looking, there were numerous other incidents that almost made them give up their search for a home in the suburbs. At one point they actually found a house and placed a deposit of $1000 on it, only to discover a few days later that a mysterious fire had burned out its kitchen. An official investigation claimed an electric short had caused the

---

[1]Interview, June, 1966.

fire, but the W.'s were not convinced. After deciding on another house, the W.'s couldn't find a bank that would grant them a mortgage. The bank's excuse was that the W.'s were not earning enough to buy this house, though they had saved for years for an especially large down-payment and their monthly mortgage would have been considerably less than the rent they were paying in New Haven. Another incident stood out in Mrs. W.'s mind. Friends had informed her of a house in a nice neighborhood, but when she got there the owner was on the phone, loudly thanking (or pretending to) the real-estate agent for finding her a buyer so soon. The "for sale" sign remained on that particular house for the next fifteen months.

There was one real estate agency which always had homes to show the W.'s. But these homes were in the predominantly Negro sections of town. Many other agencies never had anything to show them.

Today, the W.'s live in their own home in Hamden, Connecticut. They bought the house through friends, not through a real-estate agency. They are generally happy in their neighborhood now and have good relations with most of their neighbors. But occasionally they find a crudely lettered "Nigger go home" sign in their front yard. It reminds them of the difficulty they had finding a home and of the people who were too scared or too prejudiced to sell to Negroes.

The White Suburbs

The W's. were almost denied housing in Hamden because they were Negroes, and there is little doubt that other Negroes have been prevented from buying homes in the suburbs. The following chart shows how successful New Haven's suburbs have been in keeping Negroes in the cities.*

Year	New Haven Negroes	Negroes in New Haven suburbs	Percentage of Negroes in Suburbs
1900	3000	300	11.0
1910	4000	400	10.0
1920	5000	500	9.8
1930	5000	1000	11.0
1940	6000	1000	11.0
1950	10000	1000	10.1
1960	22000	2000	7.7

An alarming geographic separation of blacks into cities and whites into suburbs is explained in part by discrimination against the Katherine W.'s and their families. Each year more and more black people pile into our major cities and more and more whites retreat to the suburbs. Between 1960-1966, Negroes in central cities increased by two million; the white population in the cities decreased by one million. While fewer than one-quarter million Negroes left the city during that period, over ten million whites moved into suburban America. More than one-half of the people in Washington, D.C. are black, and many other cities will soon have more

---

*Note, figures have been rounded off to nearest 1000.

black residents than white. Indeed, if this trend continues, our cities will be almost all black, surrounded by nearly all white suburbs.

Increase in Negroes		*Increase in Whites*
1950-60		
Central Cities	3.6 mil.	1.9 mil.
Suburbs	0.6 mil.	17.2 mil.
1960-66		
Central Cities	2.0 mil.	−1.0 mil.
Suburbs	0.2 mil.	10.5 mil.

Though suburban whites enter the city each day to go to work, they flee by car and commuter train in the afternoons. They leave an increasingly large Negro population to work out their own destinies in the cities, devoid of tax base or adequate housing, education, transportation, sewage collection, etc. Less than fifteen per cent of the nation's taxes are now collected in the cities; at one time the figure was seventy-five per cent. While the cities grow poorer, the suburbs gain in wealth. As the years go by, the poor and the Negroes, especially the impoverished blacks, inherit the problems of urban decay.

Discrimination in City Housing

Discrimination in housing also explains the housing problems encountered by Negroes even within the cities. Negro families get less for their rent dollar than white families. On the average, they spend the same number of dollars on rent as whites, but almost thirty per cent of New Haven's Negroes live in substandard housing and only fifteen per cent of New Haven's whites live in substandard housing. Nearly one-half of the people living in crowded conditions in New Haven are Negroes, and many more Negroes than whites pay more than the prescribed maximum 22.5 per cent of income for rent. This discrimination also prevents Negroes from owning their own homes. At every income level, a much larger percentage of whites than blacks are homeowners. The W.'s had trouble finding a home in the suburbs. The average black family cannot easily find a decent apartment to rent in the city, or good value for its rent dollar.

Urban Renewal in New Haven

Like many American cities, New Haven was decaying during the 1950's. Its Oak Street section, where John Randolph grew into manhood, was considered one of New England's worst slums. Other neighborhoods were almost as bad. No new commercial building had been constructed in the downtown section since the 1920's. As in cities all over the country, business establishments and white citizens were leaving to locate in the suburbs.

Under the administration of Mayor Richard C. Lee, New Haven began tackling the problem of deterioration as early as 1953. Supermarkets, department, clothing, and other fine stores were attracted into the once deteriorating downtown area. Highways and huge parking garages assured access for shoppers. Highrise apartments were built to house middle- and upper-income families. Renewal money was lent to people to redecorate

Chapel Square in New Haven before redevelopment.
(New Haven Redevelopment Agency)

their homes inside and out. Slums were cleared to make room for the high-ways, shopping centers, and apartments.

New Haven's renewal efforts earned it national recognition as a model, "close to the dream of a slumless city." New Haven's redevelopment administrators were offered jobs to head face-lifting efforts in other cities. More federal dollars were spent per capita in New Haven than in any other city in the country. Many of the projects helped provide New Haven with a desperately needed tax base, allowing municipal revenues to pay for necessary services, such as education, police protection, etc.

But the bulldozers that tore up New Haven also destroyed 6500 units of low income housing. And the inhabitants of New Haven's demolished buildings were often unable to find adequate housing elsewhere, for only 951 low-income units replaced those destroyed by renewal. Most of the new housing was built during the 1950's, a good deal of it for the aged. During the 1960's there was no improvement in New Haven's housing market. According to one estimate 40 per cent of New Haven's Negro families have been relocated; some families claim they were relocated five different times. Meanwhile, New Haven suffers from one of the lowest housing vacancy rates of any city in the country. There are an estimated 3000 to 4000 substandard housing units in the city. Over 300 families are

Chapel Square in New Haven after redevelopment.
(New Haven Redevelopment Agency)

awaiting relocation; the Housing Authority has a backlog of 1500 applications for low-income housing. Landlords are able to extract unreasonably high rents because the poor have no alternatives. One of every three inner city residents lives in overcrowded conditions.

Relocation: A Case History

In 1961 Mr. and Mrs. M. lived with their five children in a five-room apartment in New Haven's Wooster Square area. The M.'s are Negroes, they are long time residents of New Haven, and they had been in their Wooster Square apartment for three years. But Wooster was one of New Haven's first redevelopment areas, and when it was slated for renewal the M.'s were forced out. Family Relocation Service helped them find a six-room city-owned house on Grand Avenue, tagged for redevelopment. Nothing else was available for the M.'s in the private real estate market. The M.'s were rejected from public housing for reasons that could not be determined. Reasons for rejecting applicants include lack of adequately large apartments (the largest only have six rooms) and moral problems.

Within a year of their arrival on Grand Avenue, the M.'s were again forced to vacate. The building was torn down to make room for Interstate Highway 91, and the M.'s were located in temporary housing again. This time the apartment was too small for the family, which had grown to ten. They were then moved into public housing on Hamilton Street, but were evicted when the family became even larger. The M.'s next move was to Chapel Street — into a seven-room apartment, large enough for the family and in conformity with minimum standards. The house was condemned, however, about the same time that the Chapel area was slated for renewal. The city moved all of the tenants out of the building, and the M.'s were next located in "permanent" housing on Dixwell Avenue. Here they pay $150 rent with heat and hot water. Two sons are now working in the city and no longer live at home. An unmarried daughter was moved to a public housing project with a child. Mr. M. was injured on his job several years ago and city welfare picks up most of the rent.

Mr. W., the Family Relocation official who worked on the case, cited several problems in relocating families like the M.'s. The lack of available housing was the largest problem. Though there is decent housing in New Haven, landlords do not want to rent to black families, to large families, or to families on welfare. Consequently Relocation is forced to find homes when there is nobody willing to rent. Urban renewal agencies do not help the situation by planning new developments without consulting Family Relocation.

Part of a National Trend

Wherever it has operated, urban renewal has caused problems. If there were more problems in New Haven than elsewhere, there also was more renewal. In theory, legal safeguards are built into the renewal program; in fact, the interests of the displaced tenants are not protected. As the wrecking crews dismantle old buildings, little new housing replaces them, and the dispossessed must compete for the remaining housing. Depletion causes housing shortages, which, in turn, force up rents. Destroying slums means destroying the houses of the poor. Urban renewal and public housing have displaced over 360,000 families, and, according to several unofficial estimates, urban renewal alone will displace another 2 million households between 1965 and 1973. Since the displaced are often the poor and the black, urban renewal programs have earned the nickname of Negro removal. Renewal or removal, the programs have failed to correct the basic housing problem — an estimated 6 million housing units in the U.S. are substandard. And it has not kept the middle class in the cities or prevented businesses from locating in the white suburbs.

The Alternatives

America's housing problem — 6 million substandard units and overcrowding accompanying dilapidation in the central cities — cannot be conquered overnight. In dealing with this problem, however, the nation must chose between three strategies or courses of action. One strategy is to do no more than we are doing now. The old approach has been aimed at restoring the cities through redevelopment — saving downtown areas, but not concentrating on relocation or on housing. The poor would presumably inherit the housing abandoned by the middle class moving to the suburbs, or they crowd into buildings subdivided to accommodate them. This is the strategy of saving the central city for the middle-income resident. To make it work, more money must be spent. Even in New Haven, whites are fleeing from the central city. If national trends continue, the nonwhite inhabitants of the central cities will increase from 14.3 million in 1968 to 20.4 million in 1978.

A second city-housing strategy is to introduce a dramatic new program to improve ghetto housing and thereby enrich the life of the ghetto resident. This strategy calls for the expenditure of more money on education, on welfare, and on anti-poverty programs. In housing, it calls for ending dispersal through relocation and spending over five billion dollars annually to build 700,000 new low-cost housing units every year for the next five years. This expenditure can alleviate the housing shortage in the cities for blacks and poor whites, and simultaneously employ black or poor white workers to accomplish the job, dramatically reducing unemployment. Obviously this program would not solve all of the Negro's problems; one of its effects would be to increase the concentration of blacks by making the cities more attractive to Negroes. But, by speaking directly to ghetto housing and employment needs, this building strategy would make the city more liveable for its poor white and black inhabitants.

A third strategy for dealing with city-housing problems is to break up the ghetto. The trend toward two societies, the white suburb and the black city, can be halted only through a concerted national effort. Open housing laws, strictly enforced, would make it possible for Negroes to move into the suburbs. Incentives to attract Negroes into the suburbs could include rent and mortgage supplements, and low-cost public housing. Since more and more factories are located in the suburbs, Negroes must get out of the cities to find employment. The level of crime and violence in ghetto areas is unacceptably high and can be reduced by breaking up concentrations of the poor and the hopeless. This strategy of opening the suburbs to Negroes perhaps is no cheaper than the strategy of making the ghetto more liveable, but it is the price of ensuring an open society for black and white Americans.

Americans are unlikely to make a clear-cut choice for one of the aforementioned housing strategies. However, they must realize that the location, the availability, and the quality of housing will determine the nature of the society in which they live. Federal programs so far have not stemmed the tide toward racial separation. Over the next decade, a choice must be made, and the choice should not be made without awareness of alternatives.

QUESTIONS

1. With which parts of the following statement do you agree? Disagree? Why?

Discrimination by whites has created the housing problems Negroes now face. It is therefore the obligation of the white community to find a solution.

2. On the balance, do you think that redevelopment was a good idea for New Haven?

3. Which of the three proposed strategies for dealing with the housing problem makes more sense to you? What are its drawbacks? Why do you favor this approach despite its drawbacks?

SUGGESTED READING

Charles Abrams has written lucidly and sympathetically on Negro housing problems. See his classic *Forbidden Neighbors* (New York, 1955) and his more recent *The City is the Frontier* (New York, 1965). George and Eunice Grier's *Equality and Beyond* (Chicago, 1966) is a good summary. Woody Klein's *Let in the Sun* (New York, 1964) is the story of a tenament house and how it became a slum building. June Jacobs in *The Death & Life of Great American Cities* (New York, 1961) argues that cities are worth saving. Martin Anderson's *The Federal Bulldozer* (Cambridge, 1964) is a critical analysis of urban renewal.

chapter 7

Racial Imbalance in Northern Schools—I

Introduction

> The answer for all our national problems, the answer for all the problems of the world comes down, when you really analyze it, to one simple word — education.
>
> President Lyndon Baines Johnson, September 28, 1964

In 1954, the United States Supreme Court pronounced separate schools for Negroes and whites as "inherently unequal," for ". . . segregation of white and colored children in public schools has a detrimental effect upon the colored children." The court's decision (see Part Three, Chapter 1) applied specifically to areas where cities and counties maintained two systems of schools; one for white children, and the other for Negroes. In these areas Negroes attended colored schools even if they lived across the street from the white school. Discrimination, in these cases, was overtly practiced by the local boards of education.

In the slum ghettos of our great Northern cities, Negroes also attend schools in which they may never see any white children. In the suburbs surrounding the cities, whites attend schools in which they see no Negroes. These schools in the North are almost as segregated as those of the South. The major difference is that segregation is not overtly practiced by the boards of education. Instead, more subtle but nevertheless equally effective forms of discrimination have conspired to keep Negroes living in predominantly Negro neighborhoods, and many local schools are therefore predominantly, if not totally, Negro. While the causes of separation differ in the North and the South, the effects are similar: inferior schooling for Negro children and the separation of both Negro and white children from the wider mainstream of American life.

> As the struggle to secure the Negroes' proper place in that society gains headway and success, it becomes steadily more clear that the two great educational handicaps he has suffered — segregated schools and inferior

141

instruction—are so closely interrelated that they can be attacked successfully only when they are attacked simultaneously.[1]

Sadly, the blunt truth is that "Negro education" is generally grossly inferior to "white education" in both the North and the South; it typically involves less expenditure per child, less trained and experienced teachers, and less adequate facilities; and it often prepares Negro youth to assume only low-skilled employment befitting "the Negro's place" as decreed by white supremists.[2]

What is the state of racial segregation in schools since the Supreme Court's decision prohibiting separation on the basis of race? Harold Howe, United States Education Commissioner, had this to say in a speech to a group of principals and superintendents in June, 1966:

. . . the schools throughout the nation remain almost as segregated today as they were in 1954 when the Supreme Court decided that racially segregated education was illegal.

. . . The facts today are that a Negro youngster in an American elementary school has on the national average not much more than fifteen percent of his classmates from the majority white groups; in the Southern states the figure is nearer five percent. White high school students can expect to have nine out of ten of their classmates from their own white groups.[3]

Commissioner Howe pointed out in the same speech that the small progress made toward desegregation in the South "has been offset by increasing de facto [from the Latin meaning "in fact"] segregation in the cities in the North."[4]

Northern cities, both large and small, have been making attempts to break down racially segregated schools. The methods to accomplish desegregation have included redrawing school boundary lines, busing Negro children into white schools and whites into black schools, and pairing predominantly Negro and predominantly white schools. In almost all cases, these attempts at desegregation have created an uproar in the white community, which has opposed integration for numerous reasons, ranging from the attachment to the principle of the neighborhood school, to the low quality of many ghetto schools, and to a fear and dislike of Negroes. New Haven, Connecticut, has been one town which tried to integrate its schools because enough people in New Haven believed that Negroes and whites belong in the same schools. This chapter examines this attempt and the larger issues it raises.

Racial Imbalance in New Haven's Schools

Housing segregation in New Haven had led to de facto segregation in the city's schools. But not until 1963 was the city's attention called to this fact. On May 23, the New Haven Human Relations Council informed the

---

[1]John Fischer, "Race and Reconciliation: The Role of the School", *Daedalus,* XCV (Winter, 1966), p. 25.
[2]Thomas F. Pettigrew, "The Failure of American Education", *ADL Bulletin,* XXIII (January, 1966), p. 4.
[3]New York *Times,* June 19, 1966, p. 53.
[4]New York *Times,* June 19, 1966, p. 53.

New Haven Board of Education that five of the thirty-seven schools in the city had Negro enrollments of ninety percent or more, and that four of these schools were the most overcrowded in the city and had the least experienced teaching staffs. The board then conducted its own investigation. Its findings were reported in the March 23, 1964, edition of the *New Haven Register:*

> Thirty-eight percent of New Haven's schools' students were nonwhite. 3 out of 8 of New Haven's Negroes attended five of the thirty-seven schools. The Negro-white ratio in these schools was twelve to one. Two schools in New Haven had no Negro enrollment. Five other schools had fewer than six Negroes enrolled.

The Board's Commitment to Racial Balance

Even before completing its survey of racial imbalance in the New Haven schools, the Board of Education issued a public statement committing itself in principle to integrating the New Haven schools.

> The New Haven Board of Education concurs in the principle that racially imbalanced schools are educationally unsound. Recognizing the fact that housing patterns have resulted in racial imbalance in certain of the New Haven schools, the Board resolves to seek for adoption a feasible plan or plans designed to provide intermingling of pupils from a broad spectrum of racial, as well as social and economic backgrounds.[5]

Meanwhile, the board began perfecting a plan to translate the above principle into reality. The plan was scheduled for release late in June, 1964, but was leaked to newspapers a few weeks earlier. Its main features included:

> 1. Altering the feeder system of elementary to junior high schools. No longer would students from the Negro elementary schools be the whole population of the virtually all-Negro Bassett Junior High School. Instead, Basset and other junior high schools would receive both black and white pupils evenly mixed.
>
> 2. All of the town's elementary schools were to be grouped into six educational districts, or clusters. Children in each of these districts were assigned schools in their neighborhoods, but could request transfer to any school in the district providing this transfer would further racial balance. The city would provide transportation to achieve this.

In its final form, the plan meant busing, for racial purposes, 850 out of 20,000 students in the schools. It meant reducing the Negro population at Bassett Junior High from more than ninety percent to approximately fifty percent by balancing it with predominantly white Sheridan Junior High. It gave parents of Negro elementary school students the opportunity of sending their children to predominantly white schools. 232 students took advantage of this opportunity in the plan's first year.

The board's plan was the center of furious discussion for over six weeks, and because of the pressure of certain white parents was modified before

---

[5]Human Relations Council of Greater New Haven, Inc., *Final Report on Grants Received from Community Progress, Inc. and the Greater New Haven Foundation, December 1, 1963 to August 31, 1965* (mimeographed copy), p. 49.

final acceptance.* The whites most opposed to the plan were those living in the elementary school districts scheduled to move into formerly Negro junior high schools, like the Bassett school. Parallel to this, there was also vehement opposition from parents of students in the formerly predominently white schools like Sheridan who would have to accept Negroes. The debate over the board's plan was frequently emotional, and involved issues ranging from the importance of the neighborhood school to the quality and meaning of democracy in America. Public meetings were held at which parents in favor of and opposed to the busing proposal could air their views. These meetings became a forum for strong arguments, heated emotions, and name-calling. But it should be noted that during angry racial quarrels there were several statements like that made by a white postman who quietly said he wanted his children to attend school with every kind of child because "this is a democracy." The printed word does not convey the depth of feeling that accompanied each statement, but as you read excerpts from the public hearings at Bassett Junior High, try to imagine the murmurs of approval and disapproval in the highly charged atmosphere that prevailed. †

The Arugments Pro and Con: Need for Busing

One woman saw no need for busing:

> All the proposals stem from the premise that racially unbalanced schools are educationally unsound. This may be a foregone conclusion, but you have to prove it to me. . . . You owe it to the parents of the displaced children to tell us how this conclusion was reached.[6]

Another parent felt that Negro schools were consciously made inferior:

> And what reason can there be now that most of the predominantly Negro schools are still being neglected. Three thousand children almost forgotten under these board proposals.
> What can the Negro parent, Negro children . . . think but that the power structure really doesn't care, the parents and taxpayers associations don't care, if another generation of Negro children go uneducated and unfulfilled? What else can one think — that the opposers of this plan would rather pay the costs of welfare, crime, and unemployment than allow an improvement in the educational system which means that their children would sit next to a child of darker skin?[7]

---

*The major modification forced by white objections: dropping the predominently Negro Winchester school as a feeder school for the predominently white Fair Haven Junior High.

†The statements have been arranged in dialogue form to convey the sense of argument at the meeting, though actually each side was given a half hour to present its viewpoint and another half hour to rebut the opposition.

[6]New Haven Board of Education, Public Hearings, *Proposals for Promoting Equality of Education and Dealing with Problems of Racial Imbalance,* Bassett Junior High School, New Haven, Connecticut, June 27, 1964 (Post Reporting Service, mimeographed copy), pp. 4-5.

[7]Public Hearings, pp. 31-32.

One woman thought the answer was to improve the schools:

> We feel that if to your thinking some schools are not up to as high a standard as other schools, then it is your job to bring these schools up to par and not up to the taxpayers to bus their children to the substandard schools and do your job for you.[8]

A high school student thought there is more to education than books:

> I represent a city-wide group of individuals, junior and senior high school students, who support the proposals of the Board of Education.
> We feel that education entails more than simply the subject of the classroom. Education to us is preparation for living and working with other people.
> For proper preparation, we feel that we must study and grow with people of all races and backgrounds. Therefore, we support the proposals of the Board of Education to correct racial imbalance in the public schools.[9]

The Rights of the Children

A father didn't want his children shuffled around the city:

> We have, in fact, overlooked the children themselves. They have become a pawn, a deck of cards, so to speak. And now you propose to shuffle them from one end of the city to another.
> I have two daughters, one now in Woodward Elementary School. I live three blocks away from the school. I want her to attend the school of her choice, as she is guaranteed that right.[10]

A mother didn't want outsiders to use her children for a racial experiment:

> The permanent residents of our city live where they are because of the children they have or have had. Too many people who are in our city for the short time of two or three years of learning, teaching or working are too willing to use our children and our tax dollars as an experiment that has failed in other cities. Let the do-gooders and the University use their own families in the experiment. Let the University raise their quota of Negroes for the admittance themselves. These people have no right to start a project, let it get out of control and then leave the voters of New Haven to finish it.
> I for one will not let these window-shoppers use any children as guinea pigs while they move to what they think are greener pastures . . . (applause)[11]

One man opposed the air of hostility:

> . . . I think that we in New Haven have witnessed something that we did not know was here. We did not know that we had this hostility in New Haven. (applause) We thought that this type of hostility only existed in the South. But I was not surprised. I don't think the Negro community was surprised, either . . .[12]

Another mother wanted to keep her children in her own community:

> . . . I am opposed to this proposition because I have to bus my children. . . . I think children should be kept in their own community. I do not think you will

[8]Public Hearings, pp. 6-7.
[9]Public Hearings, p. 52.
[10]Public Hearings, p. 8.
[11]Public Hearings, p. 12.
[12]Public Hearings, p. 19.

be serving a purpose that you are trying to serve. I think that if you correct racial imbalance by correcting segregated housing, you will then have integrated schools.

School Integration Through Integrated Housing

... Once you have integrated housing, you will automatically have integrated schools. And you are not going to accomplish the purpose you are trying to achieve by busing children from one neighborhod to the other. (applause)[13]

The chairman of the Commission on Equal Opportunities saw a vicious cycle of discrimination:

Now, we hear very frequently from people opposing a plan like this, saying, "You shouldn't do it in the school system, you have got to look to the housing pattern." And when the proposal comes up before the Board of Aldermen for the Fair Housing Practices Ordinance, they say ,"You don't do it in housing, you have to do it in employment." (applause)

And the very same people, when the Equal Opportunities Ordinance was proposed, have said, "You don't do it in employment, you do it in education." (applause)

In a sense, they are right. It has got to be done in all these fields. . . .[14]

A Catholic thought the school, like the church, should be rooted in the neighborhood:

Now I speak as a Catholic. I was aghast at this. If you are a Catholic, you know if you belong to St. Aden's Parish you don't go to St. Brendan's Parish, because it is not allowed. This is a neighborhood church, a neighborhood school.[15]

A representative of CORE didn't believe the proposals went far enough:

The Board of Education's proposals suggest many important steps towards improving New Haven schools for all children — black and white. However, we feel that these proposals do not go far enough. While the Board's plan gives some temporary benefits to some pupils in the upper primary grades, we submit that these improvements are too little and too late. By almost entirely neglecting the poor situation in the elementary schools, a whole new generation of Negro children will again be compelled to attend inadequate, segregated schools.

In particular, we feel that [the proposal] is completely ineffective and may actually promote segregation because:

(1) The district clusters on which the plan is based are themselves racially imbalanced. For example, District 3 is totally white, District 4 is predominantly Negro.

(2) Under the . . . Plan, there will be some three hundred spaces available for Negro children in predominantly white schools. However, there will be only ten spaces available to white children in Negro schools. This leaves three thousand Negro children in segregated schools.[16]

How Much Desegregation

While New Haveners were arguing and implementing racial balance in the schools, the Negro school population in the city was increasing dramati-

[13]Public Hearings, pp. 9-10.
[14]Public Hearings, p. 56.
[15]Public Hearings, p. 11.
[16]Public Hearings, p. 65.

cally. This has practically nullified the desegregation achieved by busing and pairing. The following charts record these facts:[17]

Elementary Schools:

	In New Haven						In ten suburban towns	
	1963		1964		1966		1966	
Percent Negro*	#	%	#	%	#	%	#	%
0– 33	18	58	16	52	14	43	71	97
34– 66	8	26	7	22	9	27	2	3
67–100	5	16	8	26	10	30	0	0
	31	100	31	100	33	100	73	100

Junior High Schools: In New Haven	*Percent Negro and Nonwhite in:*		
School	1963	1964	1966
Bassett	91	59	closed
Fair Haven	13	23	26
Sheriden	17	32	44
Troup	55	61	73
totals	38	42	

An Open Question

New Haven residents have watched this experiment in increased integration closely. It is still a hot topic, but almost all objective observers agree that integration has made no difference one way or the other in the performance of either white or black children in standard test scores. The real test of its worth then has to come in the area of social relationships and in the achievement of equality.

Where teachers welcomed the bused children, the newcomers felt at home. Unfortunately, some tactless teachers made bused students very uncomfortable, as did one who informed her classes that the children on the buses didn't do their homework. The problems of teaching slum children, however, run much deeper than a question of manners and tact. Teachers instructing disadvantaged children for the first time need special training and instructional materials. They need to develop a sensitivity to the problems and the special strengths of the ghetto children. Unfortunately, not all teachers were able to make the needed adjustments.

Students achieved integration more readily than their teachers or their parents. When not exposed to adult prejudice the children naturally practiced equality. Color became an identifying characteristic only — like tallness or red hair. A parent hearing that Jimmy was coming to spend the night did not know whether Jimmy was a black friend or a white one. Another immeasurable effect on the students was on their motivation to learn. This is also an intangible item, for who can measure with precision the feeling expressed by one Negro boy who never worked hard before "all

---

*Includes Puerto Rican and other non-white minorities.

[17]New Haven Public Schools, New Haven, Connecticut, *Comparison of Racial Distribution in New Haven Schools,* 1963, 1964, 1965 (mimeographed copy) and ibid. for 1966.

those white kids came in and started making off with" all the top academic honors.[18]

Behind the issue of mixing white and black students in schools is the school's purpose in a democracy. Should the schools exist primarily to prepare students for their careers? Or should they also be used to further the quest for racial equality in the nation? This is the question the people of New Haven have debated since the summer of 1963, and this is the question the nation must continually ask itself. On the answer hinges not only the Negro's place in the land of equality, but the very meaning of democracy in America.

QUESTIONS

1. On the basis of the evidence available to you, do you believe that the New Haven schools failed to provide equality of educational opportunity for its black citizens prior to the initiation of the busing program?

2. Select a statement from the New Haven Board of Education hearings and be prepared to defend it.

3. Given the failure of New Haven to obtain racial balance in its schools, what further steps, if any, would you advocate the city take to achieve equal education for all of its students?

SUGGESTED READING

William Lee Miller includes a chapter on racial imbalance in New Haven in *The Fifteenth Ward and the Great Society* (Cambridge, 1966). James Conant, while recognizing the Negro's problems in the slum schools, claims in *Slums and Suburbs* (New York, 1961) that integration in the big cities is impossible. The most comprehensive survey of unequal educational opportunities is presented in United States Department of Health, Education, and Welfare, Office of Education's *Equality of Educational Opportunity* (Washington, 1966). The report finds a small positive effect on Negroes' achievement scores when schools are integrated. Two recently published books that dramatically expose the failure of city schools in educating ghetto children are Jonathan Kozol's *Death at an Early Age* (Boston, 1967) and Herbert Kohl's *36 Children* (New York, 1967).

---

[18]Interview with Lee High School student, May, 1967.

chapter 8

Racial Imbalance in Northern Schools-II

Introduction

In a land that values education highly, Negro children are faced with the fact that their educational opportunity is not equal to that of white children. Two programs designed to achieve this equality have been attempted in New Haven. One program is aimed at improving the quality of the Negro schools through compensatory educational services like Operation Head Start, which looks to the day that such attention to the deprived students will take place within the school system. Another attempted solution is busing Negro students outside of the city and into the suburbs. Since both of these programs are either being tried or may be tried in other parts of the country, they will be examined in this chapter. The reader is asked to decide what steps should be taken to equalize educational opportunities.

Operation Head Start on Dixwell Avenue

The building at 98 Dixwell Avenue is an old structure built with sturdy bricks around the turn of the century. On Sundays, it serves as the community house for the Dixwell Avenue Congregational Church. On Mondays through Fridays, however, the community house is rented by the New Haven Board of Education. Fifteen chairs are arranged in the center of its gym every weekday morning, each marked with the first name of a pre-school youngster. Several low tables stand in back of the chairs with paints, papers, crayons, and other materials for the pre-schoolers' use.

Long before the two-hour morning schedule is slated to start, Negro boys and girls roam around the gym, handling the toys and chasing after each other. They run up to visitors, sit on their laps if given the hint of an invitation, and are quick to ask questions like "What's that suitcase for?" (pointing to my briefcase), "Are you going to stay and play with us?", or to volunteer information, "We walked out to the park yesterday."

These boys and girls are participating in an educational experiment known as Operation Head Start. Funded by the federal government, Operation Head Start operates in many parts of the country. In Mississippi, the project

Pre-kindergarten programs in New Haven.
(Summer Head Start Program, New Haven Board of Education)

is run by local Negroes who are themselves learning the subjects as they teach their children. In New Haven, the Head Start program is under the direction of the New Haven Board of Education. Its purpose is nothing less than overcoming the cultural gap which separates the Negro slum child from his white middle-class neighbor.

The Cultural Gap and Operation Head Start

In recent years, educational research has revealed secrets about human potential for learning which have exploded myths of long standing. An individual's intelligence, as measured by I.Q. tests, was once believed to be fixed and unalterable. Now scientists tell us that the mind is like a muscle and unless constantly exercised never develops properly. Psychologists know that a child's intelligence is shaped by his environment, that is, by the educational opportunities he has at home and at school.

In most cases, the parents of a Negro child growing up in a slum rarely have the time or the inclination to correct his speaking habits; consequently, he does not learn to distinguish between sounds. He is not taught to use his hands to draw; consequently, he never develops the proper hand-eye coordination so important to writing. He is not given toys that stimulate his imagination; consequently, his mind is dulled and his ability to concentrate is limited. When this child enters school his poor English, his inability to distinguish between sounds, his poor hand-eye coordination, and his short attention span conspire to make school learning difficult if not impossible. As a result, many slum children, both Negro and white, never learn how to read properly, and this failure right at the beginning of their schooling forms attitudes toward school which make correcting these problems even more difficult as they get older. The gap between slum and middle-class children generally increases as the years progress.

Operation Head Start attempts to remedy these problems before it is too late. The program provides a stimulating environment which makes up for the neglect at home. Children are taught words, colors, and directions. They are taught to play games, to paint, and draw. They learn to enjoy school, and they learn to learn. In this way they are prepared to compete in school with children from better homes.

An Interview with Mrs. Cohen at Operation Head Start

When I first talked with Mrs. Lilian Cohen at Operation Head Start, the 1965-66 school year had just ended and a summer session was about to begin. Mrs. Cohen had run the program at the Dixwell Avenue center and was eager to talk about the year. I was particularly interested in her explanation of the program's purpose, its methods, and its success. Here is some of what she had to say:

> As I see it we are getting these children ready for kindergarten, for school, and for a rich life. These children are from low income homes, many come from large families, many don't leave their apartments very often, many seldom travel beyond the block on which they live. As a result they have not had the kinds of experiences that most middle-class children have. There are so many children living in crowded apartments that their mothers do not have the time or the patience to teach them anything. They don't talk very much to them, and they don't show them how to do things, and it is therefore not surprising that they are behind the more advantaged child.

> My main object in the pre-kindergarten program is to make these children feel more comfortable and not be afraid of school because once they are at ease, I can teach them. We allow the greater part of the day for the children to move freely about the room, exploring, discovering, socializing and manipulating various materials. Only when they feel comfortable about school will they begin to talk and learn. I have had children in my classes who did not talk to anyone for several months. We praise everything they do because they are so unused to reassurance that they have little confidence in themselves. Once they have developed this confidence they have the incentive to learn.

> A simple task like holding a pencil and writing on the line is developed through constant exercise which our children do not get at home. Some do not have pencils, crayons, clay, or play-doh at home, and therefore do not learn to develop the muscles in their fingers and their eyes. Without special training, they will do badly in kindergarten and first grade. They fail in school and things rapidly go from bad to worse, because when you keep failing you lose hope and give up. We therefore spend a great deal of time teaching how to hold crayons, to paint, to use your hands in many different ways, and therefore develop abilities necessary for success in school.

Our children come from disorganized homes. We try to teach them order, neatness, and obedience. They are taught that each thing has its place, even their blocks must be stacked according to size and color. We teach them to take orders, because these children must be prepared to sit and listen, to wait their turn, and to get along in a group. Advantaged children learn these things at home. These children do not, and therefore must be taught in school. If they do not learn this in kindergarten, they move on to first grade where the teacher is surrounded by thirty or forty kids and cannot take the time to instruct each child.

There is no scientific proof that the program has been a success, but we do notice terrific progress during the year. Kids start our program unable to take care of their things, unable to identify colors, unable to use a crayon, and unable to enjoy school. By the end of the year, their attitudes are much more positive and they have learned to do all these things well. From the kindergarten teachers we hear that the children are eager to attend school, and that they are able and willing learners. They can take directions and are much more able to communicate — even their attendance records are much better. One of my groups was tested in the beginning of the year, and again six months later. Their intelligence scores increased between 12 and 23 points.

The pre-kindergarten program has been expanding every year since it was started. Last winter we had sixteen or seventeen schools in New Haven; next year we will have twenty schools and reach over 600 kids. Each year our program gets richer. Last year medical help was available for the first time; this year medical and psychological help was available. The pre-kindergarten in New Haven is so valuable, I feel it should be extended to all middle-class children. If some of the youngsters whose parents work could enter this program, I think we would have fewer dropouts when they get to junior and senior high school.[1]

Busing and the Suburbs

Operation Head Start is one way of bridging the educational gap between ghetto children and middle-class white children. There is no proof yet that it can succeed and there is considerable reason to doubt that it can completely compensate for the lack of educational opportunity in the home.* The child, after all, is in the home long before he enters school. Nor can Operation Head Start overcome the inferior education which many ghetto children obtain in the city schools' elementary grades. Schools in the suburbs are generally far superior to the city schools because they have more money for books, teachers, and buildings. And the child bused to such a school gains the advantage of attending schools where the desire to learn is transmitted by children from homes in which education is stressed to children from homes where it is not.

Passionately believing in the need to expose ghetto children to middle class values, competition, and superior schools, a group of concerned citizens in New Haven formed the Committee on Metropolitan Education. The purpose

---

[1]Interview with Lilian Cohen, June, 1966.
*A 1966 study indicated that the advantages of the Head Start program tend to disappear as the child moves on through higher grades (see *New York Times*, October 22, 1966).

of this group was to narrow the physical and psychological distance between ghetto and suburb, by busing inner city children into suburban schools. Their proposal was similar to one instituted around Hartford, Connecticut where several towns agreed to take a limited number of younger children from the inner city and to educate them in their schools. State aid and city taxes provided the necessary financing. Teachers and special education personnel accompanied the city students to the suburbs. Suburban schools accepted city students on a space available basis and never took more than three city students into any one class. The students themselves were selected at random, not according to ability, and no one was forced to attend the suburban school.

William Lichten and Courtland Wilson, chairmen of New Haven's Committee on Metropolitan Education, explain their reasons for organizing this program:

> The city and suburbs of New Haven are faced with a severe case of *de facto* [in fact] racial segregation. The cause of this condition is rooted in the soil of city poverty, middle-class suburbs, and housing discrimination. The fruits of this growth is an unhealthy separation of people from each other. Both races are harmed. Segregated education is inferior. Children who only learn to get along with others like themselves are not prepared to go out into the larger American society. This holds for both the white child in the suburb as well as for the Negro child in the city ghetto.
>
> We know only one way to have an immediate effect on this problem. This is to bus Negro children to suburban schools. Other means have been tried and have failed. . . .[2]

Opposition to Busing

Busing children from the inner city to the suburbs presents many difficulties. The suburban schools are often reluctant to take Negro slum children and this reluctance frequently turns into violent opposition. Behind the refusal to accept a few Negro children may lie the fear that busing will lead to total integration of city and suburb and force the white child to attend the inner-city school.

The Negro community also may oppose busing. Many Negro parents do not want their children sent to a hostile suburban environment where the children could be mistreated or derided. Negroes often resent the implication that black children cannot receive a decent education unless they attend school in the company of whites. Some educators and parents of both races feel that Negroes would be better served by good schools in their neighborhoods than by good schools in other areas.

The traditional argument against the slum school is that it has not satisfactorily served the needs of the Negro community. However, steps have recently been taken to correct this weakness. Operation Head Start has

---

[2]Courtland Wilson and William Lichten, *C.O.M.E., A Program to Relieve the Effects of Racial Segregation in the New Haven Metropolitan Area* (mimeographed copy).

helped pre-kindergarten children prepare for school. Ghetto schools have been upgraded with better teachers, materials, and techniques. The ghetto school can become not only a place of learning, but the center for the entire community with doors open day and night to serve the recreational as well as the educational needs of the neighborhood. These schools could improve the neighborhood and provide a secure base from which the slum child can grow confidently.

Most city schools fail to adequately serve the many needs of their students, just as the home environment has failed to prepare them satisfactorily for either school or adult life. The larger issue this chapter raises, therefore, is whether the schools should attempt to equalize educational opportunities for the slum child, and if this goal can best be accomplished within the inner city or in the suburbs.

QUESTIONS

1. Are children raised in ghettos less intelligent than children raised in suburbs?

2. Since cities generally do not have enough money to finance compensatory programs such as Operation Head Start, should the national and/or suburban governments help assume the responsibility?

3. Which is the best tool for equalizing the educational opportunity for inner city children: the bus or the improved ghetto school?

SUGGESTED READING

The Office of Economic Opportunity publishes numerous pamphlets on Operation Head Start. One of the most useful for students is *Project Head Start, Daily Program 1*. Recent books on the subject include Edward W. Gordon and Doxey Wilkerson's *Compensatory Education for the Disadvantaged* (New York, 1966) and Maya Pines' *Revolution in Learning: the years from birth to six* (New York, 1967).

chapter 9

Watts—the Ghetto Erupts

Introduction

Mob violence is not new to the American story — the first strides toward independence in the 1760's were accompanied by the tarring and feathering of British officials and their sympathizers. Nor is racial violence a new commodity. White mcbs have on many occasions roamed our major cities — New York in 1863 and in 1943, Chicago in 1919, Memphis in 1866, to name but a few cases — burning, looting, and killing Negroes. But during the 1960's, Americans have seen Negroes riot in New York City, Philadelphia, Detroit, Chicago, Newark, Jersey City, and Watts. And there are few experts on race relations who dare predict there will be no more such incidents.

All of these violent outbursts of the 1960's have taken place in the Negro ghettos of our cities. And though they were generally sparked by an incident involving white policemen arresting or manhandling young Negroes, their underlying causes were rooted in the unemployment, hatred, despair, and lawlessness so common to the Negro ghetto community. This chapter examines the most fearful of these riots and provides the reader with an opportunity to understand its causes and to prescribe remedies.

Watts Before the Riots

To the casual observer Watts was a drab section of south Los Angeles, California. Its clapboard houses and stucco buildings were plagued by peeling paint, but were pleasantly located among green lawns and palm-lined streets. When compared to the decaying tenements and garbage-littered sidewalks of some parts of Harlem or South Side Chicago, Watts did not look like a slum.

But closer investigation would have revealed some pertinent information about Watts. Its population is ninety percent Negro. Many of its pleasant, one- or two-bedroom houses are shared by two and even three families. About one out of three adults in Watts is unemployed. So many receive some kind of welfare that food prices rise the day welfare checks arrive. Nearly one-half of the men have police records; in 1964, 17,000 offenses were reported in the police precinct containing Watts.

Watts has become a stopping place for Negroes migrating from Southern farms and towns. About 2,000 come to Los Angeles every month to escape the poverty, boredom, and oppression of Southern life. But, unprepared for urban life, they are unable to get jobs and unable to get out. As these Southern Negroes crowd into Los Angeles the least successful drift into Watts and are held as in a huge wall-less prison.

The city's public transportation system (one of the worst in the nation) imprisons the Watts Negro. The bus trip to the General Motors plant, one of the large employers, is 22 miles from downtown Watts; it takes 4 hours and 45 minutes, and the roundtrip fare is $1.76. Other places of employment are almost as far away and frequently more expensive to reach. Since few of Watt's families (14 percent) own their own cars, too many find it easier to live on welfare than to spend their earnings and their time traveling to and from work.

An inferior education and the lack of job skills also conspire to keep Watts's Negroes penned in their ghetto, for few are equipped to meet the demands of today's job market. Two out of every three adults have not completed high school; many teenagers drop out of school while in junior high; one out of eight can neither read nor write. (When an employment agency was finally opened in Watts, only 400 applicants out of 4000 were hired.)

As automation eliminates jobs once performed by unskilled laborers, unemployment increases and conditions get worse. This is particularly true for the Negro. National income has soared in the United States since 1959. But Negroes in Watts have not shared in this prosperity; income there has actually decreased by 8 percent between 1959 and 1965.

Although almost cut off from the white world, Watts residents are constantly reminded of it. The TV screen is a window into the world where "whitey" enjoys the luxuries of life which are denied to the Watts Negro. The white policemen are always on the beat or cruising by car, watching out for Negro crime. The white landlords collect the rent. The white welfare workers come by to eliminate cheating on welfare; the white politicians make decisions and pronouncements that determine the destiny of Watts residents. And somewhere in the background are the concessions won from the white world by the followers of Martin Luther King, Jr., and other civil rights leaders; but they do not improve the standard of living in Watts.

The Spark that Ignited the Powder Keg

Marquette Frye, possibly a little drunk, was speeding home when he was stopped by a policecar on the corner just two blocks from his home in Watts. Shortly before 7 P.M., Wednesday, August 11, 1965, one officer subjected Frye to a "field" test for drunkenness which he failed, and told him he would be arrested and the car impounded. A crowd of twenty-five to fifty gathered. Frye smiled and tried to joke the officer out of the arrest. Suddenly, Frye's mother appeared, berated her son, and cursed the policeman, whereupon Frye became furious and called the policeman names, screaming that he wasn't going to jail. The arresting officer unholstered his pistol. "Go ahead, kill me," Frye shouted.[1] A second officer pulled out a shotgun and pointed it menacingly at the crowd. Frye was finally handcuffed and hustled into the police car. He continued to struggle, twice tried to escape, and was finally clubbed while in full view of the gathering crowd.

By this time the police had called for reinforcements and nearly fifty officers had arrived. The crowd, too, had grown in size, and, though still under control, was insulting and taunting the police. An order came for the police to retreat to avoid further trouble. But at this crucial moment, two policemen darted into the crowd and dragged out a woman who they claimed had spit on them, whereupon the crowd began scuffling with the police to free the new prisoner. Word spread like wildfire that the police had manhandled a pregnant woman (she wasn't, though a loose garment she wore made her appear pregnant), and stones were thrown at the retreating officers. The last policemen left under a hail of rocks and debris.

When the police returned to the scene, the crowd numbered more than 1500, and bricks, rocks, and bottles were flying in all directions. The police tried containing the mob in a two-block area. Their attempts were futile, and their efforts to arrest the ringleaders, or the most violent, only succeeded in stirring the crowd to more violence. Before the evening ended, fifty vehicles, including two fire trucks, were overturned, burned, or damaged; nineteen policemen and sixteen civilians were injured; and thirty-four people, including Marquette Frye, were arrested.

The Revolution Spreads

The next afternoon, the late, outspoken Los Angeles police chief, William Parker, commented on the causes of the riots:

> One person threw a rock, and then, like monkeys in a zoo, others started throwing rocks.[2]

That night (Thursday) the rioting was much worse. A Negro salesman, pressed into service by the *Los Angeles Times,* gave an account that ran something like this:

Every time a car with whites in it came down the street . . . word spread like lightning . . . "Here comes whitey — get him." As the older people stood in the background urging them on, boys and girls in their teens and men and women in their twenties, would rush into the streets and pull whites from their autos, beat them, and set fire to their cars. A white couple in their sixties were stopped and beaten as the Negroes in the background chanted, "Kill! Kill!" Flying rocks knocked a car driven by whites off course and it plowed into a parked vehicle. The mob swarmed over the whites and beat them so badly that one man's eye was left hanging out of its socket while the crowd in the background screamed, "Kill! Kill!" Several Negro ministers intervened and carried the men into an apartment, then called an ambulance,

[1]"Races", *Time,* LXXXVI (August 20, 1965), p. 16.
[2]New York *Times,* August 14, 1965, p. 8.
[3]New York *Times,* August 14, 1965, p. 8.

and the crowd turned its venom on them: "hypocrites, traitors to your race."[3] As the crowd was spitting on the ministers, Negro policemen interfered to rescue them, and drew the mob's uncontrolled wrath.

When "whitey" no longer could be found, the crowd began to turn on cars driven by Negroes. Meanwhile, fires were being set, and rocks and gunfire prevented fire engines from dousing the flames. The crowd had the upper hand and knew it. The Negroes knew the white police were terrified by their onslaught; they knew that whites were afraid, and indeed whites in other neighborhoods, fearful of the Watts uprising, were running to stores to buy guns. That evening Police Chief Parker, realizing the mob could not be controlled by the Los Angeles police, called for the National Guard.

Watts, August, 1965. *(UPI)*

From Rioting to Looting

Even the National Guard could not put down the rebellion immediately. Jeeps rolled down the streets of Watts, soldiers sat alert with machine guns ready. But no sooner was the mob pacified in one area than rioting and looting started somewhere else. And, during the day when the guard returned to camp, looting broke out again. A *New York Times* correspondent reported that on Saturday morning he could see a "smattering of people" emerge from side streets as daylight broke. "As the sun rose in the smoke-filled skyline" looting began at "full pace." The police stayed out of the area except to set road blocks for firemen. The streets filled with traffic as daylight brought out the curious, the sightseer, and the looter. Looters rushed past one another, from stores to homes, glancing around to see what others had taken. The bolder backed their cars right up to stores and loaded furniture, appliances, etc., while their vehicles were blocking traffic. Some ran home with stolen clothes and reappeared in the streets moments later wearing them. Three and four-year-old children trailed after parents laden with stolen merchandise. The streets were littered with glass, and the splinters from shattering windows cut into arms and feet, drawing blood from the looters, who barely took notice. One woman scarcely paused as she walked

Watts, August, 1965.   *(Wide World Photos, Inc.)*

---

⁴New York *Times,* August 15, 1965, p. 79.

through a plate-glass window she assumed was already broken. In the background, smoke rose from buildings still on fire; water from fire-fighting equipment ran down the gutters, and the streets were strewn with bricks, bottles, and rocks from the night's melee. Stores everywhere stood bare.

The atmosphere was one of gaiety. Jazz music blared from the nightclubs which had not been damaged because signs like "Soul brother owns this" or "Our Blood" had warned rioters that the establishment was Negro owned. The people laughed and joked; they were thoroughly enjoying themselves, taking what they felt was rightfully theirs anyway, and pleased to have thrown a scare into "whitey" the night before.

Assessing Damages

Before it was all over the five days of rioting had cost thirty-four lives, twenty-nine of them Negro, and left more than 1000 people injured. Property damages have been variously estimated between $40 to $60 million. About two-thirds of the near 4000 arrested during the riots either never had police records or had been arrested only for petty crimes. This was the aftermath of one of the most destructive riots in our nation's history. And even before it was over, people had started asking what caused it.

The Cause of the Riot

Police Chief Parker thought the riot was caused by a disrespect for the law. This he blamed on the civil rights movement which had often preached disobedience to unjust laws:

> You can't keep telling them [Negroes] that the Liberty Bell isn't ringing for them and not expect them to believe it. You can not tell people to disobey the law and not expect them to have a disrespect for the law. You cannot keep telling them that they are being abused and mistreated without expecting them to react.[5]

Former President Eisenhower also blamed street violence in Watts on the civil rights movement, which he claimed told Negroes:

> If we like a law we obey it. If we don't we are told 'You can disobey it.'

The result, the former President said, is disrespect for all laws, which encouraged the people of Watts to do what they wanted: to loot, to burn, or to destroy.

Negro leader Bayard Rustin thought the causes of the Watts riot went far deeper than the effects of the civil rights movement:

> I think the real cause is that Negro youth — jobless, hopeless — does not feel a part of American society. The major job we have is to find them work, decent housing, education, training, so they feel a part of the structure [of society]. People who feel a part of the structure do not attack it. The job of the Negro leadership is to prevent riots before they start.[6]

---

[5]"Races", p. 19.
[6]"Negro Leaders on Violence", *Time*, LXXXVI (August 20, 1965), p. 17.

President Johnson echoed this argument in a speech delivered before a Southern audience on August 15, 1965:

> As I have said time and time again, aimless violence finds fertile ground among men imprisoned by the shadowed walls of hatred, coming of age in the poverty of slums, facing their future without education or skills and with little hope of rewarding work.[7]

And from Chicago a sociologist, Dr. Philip Hauser, warned:

> There isn't a metropolitan area in the United States, especially the fifteen or so largest, where this isn't possible.[8]

The Aftermath of the Riots

California's governor at the time of the riot was Edmund (Pat) Brown. Brown was in Europe when the violence started and arrived in the United States only shortly before Watts quieted down. He ordered an immediate investigation of conditions in Watts and the report issued after 100 days of deliberations advocated:

> ... "revolutionary" programs — massive "emergency literacy" drives, a large-scale job-training and placement center, new mechanisms for processing complaints against police, and vastly expanded mass transit facilities to permit Negroes to get to jobs around sprawling Los Angeles.[9]

An aid to Los Angeles's Mayor Yorty advocated even more help:

> What we need is something like the old WPA to provide 5,000 to 10,000 jobs for a year. This would take off some of the pressure and give us time to work toward more permanent solutions.[10]

Governor Brown asked the California state legislature to appropriate $61.5 million to enact his program. By March, 1966, the money appropriations had not yet been passed. By June, only one of the 232 buildings destroyed in the riot was rebuilt and less than ten percent of those damaged had been repaired. Less than $10 million out of the $29 million of anti-poverty money promised by President Johnson had filtered down into Watts, and the total assistance provided by the Spring of 1966 consisted of only four teen-age canteens, a legal assistance office, a state employment referral office, and aid to a group known as the Westminster Neighborhood Association. Unfortunately, the same conditions that caused that city to explode in August, 1965 still exist. Indeed, riots again broke out in Watts in March, 1966.

Self-help in Watts

One of the men who took part in the first riot was Tommy Jacquette, age 22, a family man, and a high school dropout with a prison record. Tommy was not ashamed of his role in the riot:

---

[7]New York *Times,* August 16, 1965, p. 17.
[8]"The Search for Why's", *Scope.*
[9]New York *Times,* March 20, 1966, Section 4, p. 2.
[10]New York *Times,* November 7, 1965, p. 72.

There was my chance to get out and rebel, to have people behind me and doin' something.[11]

And the rebellion taught Tommy something about his neighbors in Watts:

The man is in the same shape I'm in. If we can get together, we can communicate, can help.[12]

Tommy used this insight and helped organize a group called SLANT (Self Leadership of All Nationalities Today). With a 300-man staff serving without pay, with an office, and with a car, SLANT started pushing kids back into school to get the education needed to obtain a decent job. When Tommy's money ran out, he quit and he is now doing the same type of work for the Westminster Neighborhood Association that he had done for SLANT. The fifteen men and women working for Westminster are paid from an $800 million federal antipoverty grant. But they are the first to admit that their help to Watts is like a "Band-aid in a sieve."[13] The Watts unemployment rate still hovers around thirty percent and there is no guarantee that the youths returning to school will find work when they graduate.

QUESTIONS

1. Do you think the police should be blamed for mishandling the incident that exploded Watts?

2. The report of the President's Commission on Urban Unrest blames outbreaks such as those that occurred in Watts on white racism. To what extent is this a more or less accurate interpretation of the causes of the riot than Chief Parker's or President Eisenhower's?

3. Do you think that the Negro, or the white community, has learned any important lessons from outbreaks such as the one which occurred in Watts?

SUGGESTED READING

A vivid description of the Watts riot appears in *Time,* August 20, 1966. Thomas Pynchon's article in the *New York Times Magazine* (June 12, 1966) is actually the "Journey into the Mind of Watts" the title claims. The July 15, 1966, issue of *Life* prints generous portions of the first book about Watts, *Burn, Baby, Burn* (New York, 1966) by Jerry Cohen and William S. Murphy. Jack Shepherd sees no improvement in Watts, ten months after the rioting, "In burned-out Watts: it's now baby," *Look,* (June 28, 1966). Indespensible for understanding riots and their causes are the U.S. Riot Commission Report, *Report of the National Advisory Commission on Civil Disorders* (New York, 1968), Tom Hayden's *Revolt in Newark* (New York, 1968) and Robert Conot's *River of Blood, Years of Darkness* (New York, 1968).

---

[11]"In Burned-out Watts: it's now baby", *Look* (June 28, 1966), p. 100.
[12]"In Burned-out Watts", p. 100.
[13]"In Burned-out Watts", p. 100.

chapter 10

Black Power

The March Against Fear

He announced it as a campaign against fear. The lonely black man had been in his native Mississippi only briefly and then secretly since he was the first Negro to graduate from the state's university in 1963. Now he was announcing a solitary, 220-mile march across this state, long a symbol to Negroes of racial oppression. He would make his pilgrimage to prove to Negroes that they "could conquer the fear they felt while living and traveling in Mississippi."[1] His name was James Meredith.

James Meredith started on his personal crusade June 5, 1966, accompanied by a friend, a white minister, the vice president of the Memphis NAACP, some reporters, and a few curious children. He was followed by a white Mississippian defiantly waving a Confederate flag.

Twenty-eight miles later, at 4:15 the next afternoon, a white man holding a shotgun called to Meredith from the side of the road. Witnesses on the

James Meredith felled.   *(Wide World Photos, Inc.)*

---

[1]New York *Times,* June 6, 1966, p. 1.

scene later claimed police had two minutes in which to act. They failed to protect Meredith and a single blast from the shotgun rammed 60 to 70 pellets of buckshot into his back and shoulders. Meredith was rushed to a Memphis hospital and civil rights leaders from all over the nation flew to his bed side. Reverend Martin Luther King, Jr., came straight from a staff meeting of the Southern Christian Leadership Council. Floyd McKissick, its national director, represented the Congress of Racial Equality. Stokely Carmichael, the newly elected chairman of the Student Nonviolent Coordinating Committee, was there with his assistant, Cleveland Sellers. Though their organizations represented different approaches to civil rights, all four men agreed to take up the march at the spot Meredith was shot.

As the four civil rights leaders trudged along Meredith's route on Highway 51 they talked almost as much as they walked. And as hundreds from the North and from the South joined this pilgrimage, the talking came to center on two major issues: what was the role in the civil rights movement of the white liberal? and could whites be moved to give the Negro his due?

"We've received a lot of help from white liberals and we appreciate it," said Floyd McKissick of CORE. "But the situation is sort of like when you are sick and your neighbor comes in to help you. You need his assistance, but you don't want him to run your house or take your wife."[2]

In Batesville, Mississippi, Martin Luther King's assistant, Ralph Abernathy, told his audience:

"If you got any notion that Negroes can solve our problems by ourselves, you got another thought coming. We welcome white people." Then a pause.

"Ain't that right?"

"That's right," the audience shouted.[3]

The Birth of a Slogan

Earlier on, Stokely Carmichael had declared he was not "going to beg the white man for anything I deserve. I am going to take it." And nine days later, at a rally in Greenwood, Mississippi, Carmichael expressed his disgust with white Mississippi justice: "What we need," he proclaimed, "is black power." Moments later his assistant, Willie Ricks, leaped to the platform, demanding, "What do you want?" and the audience yelled back "Black Power." "What do you want?" Ricks asked again, and again the audience responded, "Black Power." That night the phrase *Black Power* was born as a slogan in the civil rights movement.[4]

Shortly afterwards the black power slogan was repudiated by Martin Luther King, Jr.:

> We must never seek power exclusively for the Negro, but the sharing of power with white people. Any other course is exchanging one form of tyranny for another. Black supremacy would be equally as evil as white supremacy.[5]

---

[2]New York *Times,* June 12, 1966, p. 1.
[3]New York *Times,* June 12, 1966, p. 82.
[4]Martin Luther King, Jr., *Where Do We Go From Here: Chaos or Community?,* (New York, 1968), p. 34.
[5]New York *Times,* June 21, 1966, p. 30.

Stokely Carmichael demands power for black Americans. *(Magnum Photos, Inc.)*

The debate over black power was far from over and indeed still engages the civil rights movement. At a rally in Jackson, Mississippi, which terminated the march against fear, Charles Evers and other NAACP representatives were prevented from speaking because they had not signed the March manifesto. The manifesto, among other things, had called for federal voter registrars in 600 southern counties, and billions of federal dollars to combat poverty. Evers had thought this too "radical," and likely to alienate white supporters. Meanwhile SNCC was distributing posters bearing the inscription "Move on Over or We Will Move on Over You," CORE passed out "Freedom Now" posters and SCLC handed out plastic American flags, which Willie Ricks of SNCC tried collecting, "[t]hat flag does not represent you."[6] All the time supporters of King's SCLC vied with Carmichael's SNCC in yelling "black power" and "freedom now" slogans. In their speeches, King stressed that many Negroes perish from injustice "in a vast ocean of prosperity," while Carmichael implored Negroes to "build a power base in this country so strong that we will bring them (whites) to their knees every time they mess with us."[7]

The Elements of Black Power

Perhaps symbolically, Meredith's march against fear served as the crucible for the black power slogan. Certainly, the slogan echoes across the land long after the march ended and continues to divide and confuse both black and

---

[6]New York *Times,* June 27, 1966, p. 29.
[7]*loc. cit.*

white Americans. The confusion results from the meaning of the phrase, for it is unlikely that any two black power advocates mean the same thing. To an extent, such divergent thinkers as Carmichael and King could agree on the meaning of black power, and to an extent their concepts of black power are radically opposed. Let us first examine the similarities.

Black Power, according to Martin Luther King, "in its broad and positive meaning, is a call to black people to amass the political and economic strength to achieve their legitimate goals . . . "[8] and according to Carmichael, black power means ". . . the coming together of black people to elect representatives and *to force those representatives to speak to their needs. . . .* The power must be that of a community, and emanate from there."[9]

Martin Luther King, Jr.

(Wide World Photos, Inc.)

In its economic meaning, King saw black power as a "call for the pooling of black financial resources to achieve economic security. . . . Through the pooling of such resources and the development of habits of thrift and techniques of wise investment, the Negro will be doing his share to grapple with his problem of economic deprivation."[10] Economically, for Carmichael, black power "is not merely a society in which all black men have enough money to buy the good things of life. When we urge that black money go into black pockets, we mean the communal pocket. We want to see money go

[8]Martin Luther King, Jr., *Where Do We Go From Here: Chaos or Community?,* p. 42.
[9]Stokely Carmichael, *What We Want* (mimeographed reprint from *New York Review of Books,* September 22, 1966), p. 5.
[10]Martin Luther King, Jr., *Where Do We Go From Here: Chaos or Community?,* p. 44.

back into the community and used to benefit it. We want to see the cooperative concept applied to business and banking. We want to see black ghetto
residents demand that an exploiting store keeper sell them, at minimal cost, a
building or a shop that they will own and improve cooperatively; they can
back their demand with a rent strike, or a boycott, and a community so uni-
fied behind them that no one else will move into the building or buy at the
store."[11]

And finally, psychologically, the King and Carmichael vision of black
power are quite similar. For King, "Black Power is a psychological call to
manhood . . . the Negro must boldly throw off the manacles of self-abnegation
and say to himself and the world: 'I am somebody. I am a person. I am a
man of dignity and honor. I have a rich and noble history, however painful
and exploited that history has been. I am black and comely.' "[12] Carmichael
sees black power in a similar vein, "When we begin to define our own image,
the stereotypes — that is, lies — that our oppressor has developed will begin
in the white community and end there. The black community will have a
positive image of itself that *it* has created. . . . From now on we shall view
ourselves as African-Americans and as black people who are in fact energetic, determined, intelligent, beautiful and peace-loving."[13]

The Differences

If Carmichael and King agreed on black power as a call for Negro manhood, political strength, and economic development, why then has black
power been the occasion of so much distrust, fear, and dissension? Part of
the answer undoubtedly lies in an inability of the white community to accept
Negro goals and inspiration that are not governed by whites. Another large
part of the reason may lie in assumptions and calls to action which frequently
accompany the call for black power. Probably the most frequently men-
tioned are: the rejection of integration as a goal, the explicit or implicit call
for violence, and a deep pessimism about the nature of society. In the writ-
ings of men like Carmichael and in the speeches and conversations of those
who call for black power, we trace a deep despair with the society that has
held the Negro first as servile laborer on plantations and tenant farms, and
then as virtual prisoner in black ghettos. Advocates of black power usually
reject integration into such a society, and may call for violence to effect the
kind of changes that will liberate Negroes from their white oppressors.

White Racism and Black Subjugation

The white community, Carmichael argues, has purposefully and systematically oppressed the black community:

---

[11]Stokely Carmichael, *What We Want*, p. 5.
[12]Martin Luther King, Jr., *Where Do We Go From Here: Chaos or Community?*,
pp. 44-45, & 50.
[13]Stokely Carmichael and Charles V. Hamilton, *Black Power and the Politics of
Liberation in America* (New York, 1967), pp. 37-38.

The history of every institution of this society indicates that a major concern in the ordering and structuring of the society has been the maintaining of the Negro community in its condition of dependence and oppression. This has not been on the level of individual acts of discrimination between individual whites against individual Negroes, but as total acts by the white community against the Negro community. . . .

Let me give an example of the difference between individual racism and institutionalized racism, and the society's response to both. When un-identified white terrorists bomb a Negro Church and kill five children, that is an act of individual racism, widely deplored by most segments of the society. But when in that same city, Birmingham, Alabama, not five but 500 Negro babies die each year because of a lack of proper food, shelter and medical facilities, and thousands more are destroyed and maimed physically, emotionally and intellectually because of conditions of poverty and depriva-tion in the ghetto, that is a function of institutionalized racism. . . .

It is more than a figure of speech to say that the Negro community in America is the victim of white imperialism and colonial exploitation. This is in practical economic and political terms true. There are over 20 million black people comprising ten percent of this nation. They for the most part live in well-defined areas of the country — in the shanty-towns and rural black belt areas of the South, and increasingly in the slums of northern and western in-dustrial cities. . . .

It is white power that makes the laws, and it is violent white power in the form of armed white cops that enforces those laws with guns and nightsticks. The vast majority of Negroes in this country live in these captive communities and must endure these conditions of oppression because, and only because, *they are black and powerless.*[14]

The Rejection of Integration

"The food Ralph Bunche eats," Carmichael says, "does not fill my stomach." Carmichael sees little of value for the mass of black people in the successful career of one black man, even one who becomes a key official of the United Nations. It is with this view that Carmichael sees the question of integration — the goal of moving Negroes into white society is irrelevant to most black people who do not have the money to sleep in an integrated motel or move into a white suburb. Furthermore, integration reinforces the idea that white is automatically better than black:

Integration, moreover, speaks to the problem of blackness in a despicable way. As a goal it has been based in complete acceptance of the fact that *in order to have* a decent house or education, blacks must move into a white neighbor-hood or send their children to a white school. This reinforces, among both black and white, the idea that "white" is automatically better and "black" is by definition inferior. This is why integration is a subterfuge for the main-tanance of white supremacy. It allows the nation to focus on a handful of Southern children who get into white schools, at great price, and to ignore the 94 per cent who are left behind in unimproved all-black schools. Such

---

[14]Stokely Carmichael, *Toward Black Liberation* (reprint from *The Massachusetts Review,* Autumn, 1966) (New York, 1966), pp. 4-5.

situations will not change until black people have power — to control their own school boards, in this case. Then Negroes become equal in a way that means something, and integration ceases to be a one-way street. Then integration doesn't mean draining skills and energies from the ghetto into white neighborhoods; then it can mean white people moving from Beverly Hills into Watts . . .[15]

Violence v. Nonviolence

Finally, it is not easy to document a call for violent revolution among black power advocates. True, the philosophy of Black Power developed partially over the question of using retaliatory violence in Mississippi when and if more Negroes were gunned down. Here the call to arms was clearly limited to defensive rather than aggressive measures. Furthermore, many times when leaders like H. Rapp Brown and Stokely Carmichael seem to be asking their followers to use weapons in order to make the revolution, their plea may only be a symbolic call to militancy rather than a specific call to arms. Rather than wanting to destroy America, the black militants may be trying to wake her up with their harsh words. Indeed, many advocates of black power seem to spend as much time explaining that militants don't want a revolution as they do justifying thinly veiled threats of the use of force against the "white power structure."

Nevertheless, it is disturbing to hear reports of Stokely Carmichael exclaiming, "The method of struggle for American Negroes is guerilla warfare."[16] Such a call is frightening when viewed against the violence of the ghetto and the reports of both blacks and whites arming themselves for confrontations, which extremists in both camps regard as welcome, or at least inevitable. Americans who are aware of their history know that white racists would probably field larger guerilla bands than any the black people might muster. And the call for violence in the cities is almost a logical extension of a view of society that sees whites as the constant and conscious exploiters of blacks.

White Americans are quick to blame the black men who speak stridently of the racial antagonisms of the day. They forget that many of these Negroes have long worked for cooperation with white Americans (and many continue to do so even as they call for more drastic measures). They forget too the long history of oppression of black Americans and the nation's failure to take large-scale action to correct the inequities so deeply ingrained in the American society. If violent trouble comes to America, who will be to blame — the black man who demands change or the white man who calls for maintenance of the established order?

---

[15]Stokely Carmichael, *"What We Want"*, p. 3.
[16]New York *Times,* August 2, 1967, p. 12.

QUESTIONS

1. Black power advocates often assume that: (a) The white community is unable or unwilling to make this a "land of equality." (b) The Negro can best make it alone, economically or politically, rather than by appealing for white help. (c) Whites will only respond to violence or the threat of violence. How important are each of these assumptions to your concept of black power?

2. How realistic are each of these assumptions?

SUGGESTED READING

A great deal has been written recently about Black Power. Martin Luther King, Jr., had an excellent chapter in *Where Do We Go from Here: Chaos or Community?* (New York, 1967). Full length books include Stokely Carmichael and Charles V. Hamilton's *Black Power, The Politics of Liberation in America* (New York, 1967), especially strong on the weakness of white power; Charles E. Fager's *White Reflections on Black Power* (Grand Rapids, 1967), which addresses itself to the white liberal's task; and Floyd B. Barbour's *The Black Power Revolt* (Boston, 1968), a collection of essays. This list is far from exhaustive.

chapter 11

Compensation for the Negro

Comparing Grandfathers

Debates over the Negro problem often boil down to what is known as the comparative grandfather argument. In this argument, the Negro on welfare is compared with the grandfather of a well-to-do second-generation white American. One side of the argument runs something like this:

"It is true that Negroes have been treated badly, first as slaves and then as freedmen with few political or civil rights. Negroes have therefore been ill-prepared for city life. But my grandfather also came to this country with little preparation for city life. He had been an illiterate farmer in Italy (or Poland, or Germany) and arrived in the States penniless, without even knowing the language. He worked hard, saved his money, learned English in night school, and sent his sons to college. If he and millions like him could overcome poverty, illiteracy, and discrimination, why can't the Negro?"

One answer to this argument is that the Negro was forced to come to the states as a slave; he was subjected to slavery for more than 200 years, and he still suffers from discrimination. Another is that the Negro is black, and, unlike other immigrants, cannot overcome the thing which makes him visibly different from the white majority, which has long regarded black men as inferior. The man with the ambitious grandfather, however, will reply: "Slavery ended more than 100 years ago; discrimination against colored people is now illegal; and welfare and unemployment give Negroes assistance that was not offered in my grandfather's day. And Negroes take advantage of that special assistance. They refuse to work and they live on unemployment insurance; Negro mothers collect welfare, husbands desert their wives, and the children drop out of school. These people are not prevented from finding work, from meeting their family responsibilities, or from completing school. They have more opportunities than the immigrants sixty years ago, but they fail to take advantage of them. Their lack of progress is no one's fault but their own."

The Negro's champion may point out that his friend with the grandfather does not understand the problem today: that slavery and discrimination have damaged the Negro's initiative, and left him ill-prepared for employment; that automation is eliminating the jobs whites once allowed Negroes to perform; that the ghetto breeds a sense of despair that is almost impossible to overcome. President Johnson made some of these same points at Howard University in June, 1965. He asked,

> can we find a complete answer in the experience of other American minorities? They made a valiant and a largely successful effort to emerge from poverty and prejudice. The Negro, like these others will have to rely mostly on his own efforts, but he just can not do it alone, for they did not have the heritage of centuries to overcome and they did not have a cultural tradition which had been twisted and battered by endless years of hatred and hopelessness.
>
> ... Men and women of all races are born with the same range of abilities. But ability is not just the product of birth; ability is stretched or stunted by the family that you live with and the neighborhood you live in, by the school you go to, and the poverty or richness of your surroundings.[1]

In the same speech, the President suggested a national conference of private citizens interested in the Negro problem to meet the following year and draw up a list of proposals that would give the Negro "equality as a fact and equality as a result."[2] In June, 1966 more than 2000 national leaders met in Washington and proposed a multibillion dollar program to give the Negro "true equality." The proposals went far beyond legally granting equal treatment to Negroes — they included massive expenditures to improve Negro employment, housing, and education. They again raise the issue, as did Johnson's speech, of compensation or special treatment for Negroes to make up for centuries of neglect and exploitation. This issue, whether the Negro should be given special treatment, is the subject for this chapter.

The Argument for Compensation

In October, 1963, the *New York Times Magazine* printed two articles on the subject of compensation for the Negroes. The first, by Whitney Young, argued for a ten-year program of special treatment to make up for three centuries of mistreatment. The second by Kyle Haseldon, presented the case for equality, but no more. Sections of these articles and letters to the editor are printed below:

> On an economic level, the hard but simple fact . . . is that the past of the Negro exists in the present. Citizens everywhere must realize that the effects of over 300 years of oppression cannot be obliterated by doing business as usual. . . .
>
> The facts speak for themselves. Today, the average Negro family earns $3,233, as compared with $5,835 for the white family — a difference of 45 percent. This gap has widened by two percentage points in the last decade alone. It has widened because the Negro started receiving too little, too late. More than 75 percent of Negro workers are found in the three lowest occupational categories — service workers, semiskilled workers, and unskilled and

[1]New York *Times,* June 5, 1965, p. 14.
[2]New York *Times,* June 5, 1965, p. 14.

farm labor — the categories most affected by the geometric growth of automation. These same catagories include less than 39 percent of white workers.

By the same token, one out of every six Negro dwellings is substandard, as compared with one in 32 white dwellings. One in every four Negro women with preschool children is working away from home. Of the school dropouts, 21 percent are Negro; only 7 percent of high school graduates are Negroes. Unemployment rates for Negroes are from two and one-half to three times higher than those for white workers.

To overcome these conditions the National Urban League declares that the nation must undertake an immediate, dramatic and tangible "crash program" — a domestic Marshall Plan — to close this intolerable economic, social and educational gap, which separates the vast majority of Negro citizens from other Americans.

. . . the scales of equal opportunity are now heavily weighted against the Negro and cannot be corrected in today's technological society simply by applying equal weights. For more than 300 years the white American has received special consideration, or "preferential treatment," if you will, over the Negro. What we ask now is that for a brief period there be a deliberate and massive effort to include the Negro citizen in the mainstream of American life. Furthermore, we are not asking for equal time; a major effort, honestly applied, need last only some ten years. . . .

. . . the crash programs that we propose are not an effort to impose the guilt and sins of a past generation on our present white community. This is an appeal for all Americans, working together to rid present-day America of its sickening disease and its moral shame.[3]

The Argument Against Special Treatment

Compensation must be rejected as an equalizer of competition between Negroes and whites for several reasons, all of which rest on the grounds to which the Negro appeals in his demand for freedom and equality.

First, compensation for Negroes is a subtle but pernicious form of racism. It requires that men be dealt with by society on the basis of race and color rather than on the basis of their humanity. It would therefore as a public policy legalize, deepen and perpetuate the abominable racial cleavage which has ostracized and crippled the American Negro. Racism, whoever may be its temporary beneficiary, should be eliminated from the social order, not confirmed by it.

Second, preferential economic status for Negroes would penalize the living in a futile attempt to collect a debt owed by the dead. The 20th-century white man is no more to blame for the fact that his ancestors bought and held slaves than are 20th-century Negroes for the fact that some of their ancestors captured and sold slaves. . . .

Third, . . . Preferred status for the Negro, however much society may owe him a debt, will inevitably destroy in him the initiative and enterprise required of a minority people in a highly competitive society. Slavery corrupts ambition and self-reliance; so too, does patronizing social status.

[3]Whitney M. Young, Jr., "Domestic Marshall Plan", *The New York Times Magazine,* October 6, 1963, pp. 43, 129, 131.

Fourth, compensation for Negroes would be unfair to other minorities handicapped by their history or by rapid social and industrial change: Puerto Ricans, Mexican-Americans, migrants of all races, Indians, coal miners and others. . . .

Our goal should be parity, not preferment. . . .[4]

Letter to the editor in response to Mr. Haselden

Mr. Haselden, it seems to me, overlooks the basic factor in the whole debate. Compensatory services are needed for all groups denied equality of opportunity — Mexicans, Puerto Ricans, Indians, Appalachian whites and others, as well as Negroes. In this country, Negroes form not only the largest deprived group, but also the one which has suffered the most as a result of the evils of society. . . .

. . . Mr. Haselden, after admitting that Negroes need help from the society which has handicapped them, is perfectly willing to abandon them to their own resources. It is time that we recognized that gross equality of services for all is a form of gross inequality of opportunity for many. At this moment in our history, only some form of compensatory service and assistance can give to many of our Negro citizens at least a minimum of real opportunity.[5]

Letter to the editor in response to Mr. Young

As a Negro, I feel that the Urban League's Whitney M. Young . . . is tragically wrong in his scheme for special treatment for Negroes — wrong not only tactically and morally, but wrong in terms of its probable effects on Negroes themselves. How can anyone seriously expect to develop initiative, respect for work and responsibility among people who are "sought" for good jobs, who receive "conscious preferment" and other . . . evasions meaning special privilege?

. . . Has Mr. Young ever checked the numerical representation of Negroes in free evening high schools and colleges, in public libraries and at free public concerts?

People who have been trying for years to tell others that Negroes are basically no different from anybody else should not themselves lose sight of the fact that Negroes are just like everyone else in wanting something for nothing. The worst thing that could happen would be to hold out hopes of getting it.[6]

The Problem in Larger Focus

The debate over compensatory treatment is an important one. It is widely believed that there is not much that can be enacted to end discrimination in the way of legislation. The laws are already on the books; the 14th Amendment, that guarantees "equal protection under the law" to all Americans, has been reactivated by the Supreme Court. If more is to be done for the Negro, it will have to come in the form of special programs. This task was begun by black people and white people who were determined to make it no longer an irony to speak of the black people in the land of equality. The decision to make equality a reality rests with the new generation.

---

[4]Kyle Haseldon, "Parity, not Preference", *The New York Times Magazine,* October 6, 1963, p. 128.
[5]*New York Times Magazine,* October 27, 1963, p. 76.
[6]*New York Times Magazine,* October 20, 1963, p. 6, 20.

QUESTIONS

1. Do the greater handicaps Negroes suffered sufficiently explain why many white immigrants have been able to succeed and most Negroes have not?

2. Compensatory treatment means going beyond equality of treatment to achieve equality of results. Do you think compensatory treatment should be given Negroes — should it include spending extra money on housing and educating Negroes? Should it mean giving Negroes preferential treatment in employment?

3. What different strategies would be involved in Negroes working for compensatory treatment and for Black Power? Which strategy would you advise a Negro friend to adopt?

SUGGESTED READING

The debate over compensatory treatment was presented in *The New York Times Magazine,* October 6, 1963, and covers the central issues raised in this chapter. A comprehensive plan to obtain compensatory treatment was drawn up by the White House Conference "To Fullfil these Rights", *Council's Report and Recommendations to the Conference,* and by the A. Phillip Randolph Institute *A 'Freedom Budget' for all Americans,* (New York, 1966). Both reports are available upon request. Senators Javits, Ribicoff and the late Robert F. Kennedy discuss Daniel Moynihan's proposed family allowance for the poor in "The Case for a Family Allowance", *The New York Times Magazine,* February 5, 1967.

Index

301.451
L

467